W9-DGV-372

Earth's
Changing
Climate

ENVIRONMENT AT RISK

Earth's
Changing
Climate

CHRISTINE PETERSEN

Marshall Cavendish
Benchmark
New York

Other Marshall Cavendish Offices:
Marshall Cavendish International (Asia) Private Limited, 1 New Industrial Road, Singapore 536196 • Marshall Cavendish International (Thailand) Co Ltd. 253 Asoke, 12th Flr, Sukhumvit 21 Road, Klongtoey Nua, Wattana, Bangkok 10110, Thailand • Marshall Cavendish (Malaysia) Sdn Bhd, Times Subang, Lot 46, Subang Hi-Tech Industrial Park, Batu Tiga, 40000 Shah Alam, Selangor Darul Ehsan, Malaysia

Marshall Cavendish is a trademark of Times Publishing Limited

All websites were available and accurate when this book was sent to press.

Library of Congress Cataloging-in-Publication Data
Petersen, Christine.
Earth's changing climate / by Christine Petersen.
p. cm. — (Environment at risk)
Summary: "Provides comprehensive information on Earth's climate changes. An exploration of case studies, ancient Earth's climate, its impact on Arctic regions, and recent studies are explored"— Provided by publisher.
Includes bibliographical references and index.
ISBN 978-0-7614-4006-2
1. Climatic changes—Popular works. I. Title.
QC981.8.C5P486 2011
551.6—dc22
2008043932

Editor: Christine Florie
Publisher: Michelle Bisson
Art Director: Anahid Hamparian
Series Designer: Sonia Chaghatzbanian

Expert Reader: Karl Kreutz, associate professor of earth sciences and quaternary and climate studies, University of Maine, Orono

Photo research by Marybeth Kavanagh

Cover photo by Stone/Getty Images

The photographs in this book are used by permission and through the courtesy of:
Getty Images: Johnny Johnson, 2–3; Michael Hall, 2 (bottom), back cover; NOAA, 15; Ronaldo Schemidt/ AFP, 21; David Trood, 27; National Geographic: 48; 30 (Lloyd Kenneth Townsend Jr.); 50 (George F. Mobley); Hulton Archive, 46; Topical Press Agency, 47; Dieter Spannknebel/Image Bank, 52; Thomas Kitchin & Victoria Hurst, 59; James Balog, 62; Tim Graham, 70; Wilfried Krecichwost, 71; Louis Bencze, 74; AP Photo: Ian Barrett, 6; NASA, 60 (top); NASA, National Snow and Ice Data Center, University of Colorado, Ted Scambos, 60 (bottom); Peter Dejong, 78; The Image Works: NSF/Lightroom/Topham, 10; Mary Evans Picture Library, 38; Alamy: Ninette Maumus, 16; Caro, 18; Chad Ehlers, 20; Universal Images Group Limited, 22; Buddy Mays, 28; blickwinkel, 64; Photo Researchers, Inc: Detlev van Ravens005waay, 31; Science Source, 33, 39, 54; The Bridgeman Art Library: Museum of the Jewish Diaspora, Tel Aviv, Israel, 36; The Granger Collection, NY: 40, 45; Corbis: Ashley Cooper/Picimpact, 66; Superstock: Indexstock, 80; age fotostock: Adalberto Ríos, 83

Printed in Malaysia (T)
1 3 5 6 4 2

4752

Contents

One

A World of Change

The term *climate change* appears in news media, the classroom, and even as a theme in movies and novels. It is a phrase that haunts the modern world. Climate change is such a prevalent topic that it almost seems like a part of pop culture. Yet climate change is a very real and serious issue. Scientists recognized the possibility of human-caused climate change more than a century ago and have recorded evidence of climate-changing gases since the 1950s. Reporters have told this ongoing story for more than thirty years. People are beginning to listen but often do not understand what they hear.

Climate change is the long-term alteration of Earth's patterns of precipitation and temperature. A consistent rise in global average temperatures over the past century or longer has led some to describe the pattern as "global warming." Data clearly reveal that climate change is taking place, and most scientists agree that humans have played an important role in promoting this change.

In Montreal, Canada, a crowd gathered in 2005 to protest global warming at the United Nations Climate Change Conference.

Earth's Changing Climate

The following true story illustrates how sometimes the local weather seems to suggest that global warming is far from a reality. On September 3, 2008, the second day of a new school year in Minneapolis, Minnesota, a father and his two daughters walk toward the front door of a neighborhood elementary school. Both girls are dressed in T-shirts and shorts. Both are shivering.

"Hey," comments the father as he passes lunch bags to both girls, "it's pretty chilly out here."

Half listening, the older girl responds, "Yeah, weren't you listening in the car? They said it's going to be a record low temperature or something."

"Really?" The father grins. "Well, so much for global warming."

Now the older girl is fully attentive. In an exasperated tone she replies, "Seriously, Dad! A few days of cold weather doesn't mean anything—the whole climate is changing! I did a big presentation on it in class last year."

The man puts up his hands, pretending to surrender. "It was a joke!" His voice turns serious. "Honey, I didn't mean to be disrespectful. I remember what you said in your report: Minnesota's air, soil, and water have gotten warmer this past century—and the same thing is happening in most of the world."

The younger girl reaches up to give her father a parting hug. "Daddy, would you bring me a sweater from home?"

"Don't bother, kid," quips her sister. "Enjoy the cool weather while you can."

Weather and Climate

The distinction between weather and climate is an important one to make. Weather describes the current conditions in the atmosphere at a particular location. Wind, cloud cover, precipitation, and humidity are some of its components. The fact that weather can be influenced by many factors in the environment explains why local weather forecasters have a hard time making exact predictions, despite all their training and high-tech instruments. If you want to know exactly how hot it will be at the beach tomorrow or how much rain will fall on your garden, you will just have to wait and see. Climate, on the other hand, describes the long-term patterns of weather for a given location. For example, it is a good bet that Las Vegas is not the place to look for good deals on ski packages—it is a pretty hot and dry place. No meteorologist is needed to predict that it is smart to pack a raincoat when traveling to Seattle in winter.

In Minneapolis the weather becomes a bit unpredictable in early autumn, but kids do not usually need to wear a jacket at the beginning of the school year—it is still a time to show off summer tans and enjoy comfortable, lightweight clothes. On September 3, 2008, the morning temperature of 49 degrees Fahrenheit (9.5 degrees Celsius), was colder than normal, the normal temperature being based on data collected since 1891. The following week was filled with chilly days; and when morning temperatures on September 9 dipped to 39 °F (3.9 °C), a record set in 1898 was tied. People grumbled about the need for long sleeves and pants and hoped for warmer days before the onset of their northern winter. A single week of cold weather, however, is not sufficient to alter the description of a climate— nor does it invalidate evidence that a period of global warming is currently under way.

A Case Study in Climate Change

Minnesota can provide some clues about the extent of this warming. On average, air temperatures in the state have increased by 1 to 2 °F (0.55–1.1 °C) in the past century. The rate of this increase has not been consistent—temperatures have risen faster over the past couple of decades.

Global temperature records have been collected since the 1850s, when weather stations were set up in many parts of the world. (Antarctic record keeping began much later, in 1957.) Today daily temperature readings are taken at thousands

The data taken at the Racer Rock weather station on the Antarctic Peninsula is sent to U.S. researchers via satellite.

of locations on land; ships and satellites are used to obtain temperatures on the ocean and in the atmosphere, respectively. Analysis of these data shows that between 1906 and 2005, average global temperature increased by 1.3 °F (0.74 °C). Scientists from Goddard Space Flight Center (a division of the National Aeronautics and Space Administration, or NASA) analyzed this global temperature data. They found that the century's hottest years have all taken place since 1990. The record holder is 2005, with 1998 and 2007 tied for a close second place. (If results for the United States are analyzed separately from global data, the outcome is slightly different. Three years—1934, 1998, and 2005—are statistically close enough to share the title of "hottest U.S. year.")

Temperature and precipitation are closely related, and together they have a strong influence on climate. For example, Minnesota has warm, humid summers and cold winters that are comparatively dry. (Ironically, despite its reputation for snow, most of the state's precipitation comes in the warm months.) The state is also located far inland (rather than near a coast) and at a low elevation (rather than in the mountains). These characteristics place Minnesota in climatologists' classification zone system as having a continental climate. Continental climates are found in other parts of the world that have similar geographic characteristics: throughout much of central North America, Russia, north-central Europe, and parts of China. There is also variation within the climate zone. For example, average winter temperatures are 14 °F (7.8 °C) higher at the southern end of Minnesota than at the Canadian border, about 400 miles (643 kilometers) farther north. This variation affects levels of precipitation and other aspects of weather and creates a mosaic of ecosystems across the state.

Minnesota encompasses three ecosystems that are common in the continental climate zone: prairie, northern deciduous forest, and northern coniferous forest. Prairie is generally found in locales with cold winters, hot summers, and little rain. Minnesota's southern regions match this description. Prairie grasses survive by growing long roots,

which provide access to water in times of heat and drought and allow the plants to quickly recover from wildfires. As early settlers found out, this climate is also ideal for growing grains and corn. Today it supports a large agricultural community and very little native prairie. Deciduous forest dominates the middle of the state, which is warm and gets a lot of precipitation. Maples, basswood, oak, and other deciduous trees lose their leaves each autumn. The shedding of leaves temporarily stops photosynthesis; as a result, water loss from the tree is reduced. By losing leaves, trees also decrease the surface area on which ice can gather. Consequently, there is less risk of limbs becoming broken by ice. Conifers (or evergreens), which prefer cool temperatures and plenty of rain and snow, are found in the northeastern corner.

The weather in continental climate zones is determined in part by their inland location. Large landmasses allow heat to gather in summer. The warm air forms low-pressure weather systems, which can push across the landscape over long distances. Hot air rises and causes a lot of movement in these air masses. Storms result, bringing summer rain. In winter, cold air from the Arctic produces high-pressure systems, which flow low to the ground and bring extremely cold and dry conditions. (Snowstorms may result when an Arctic high-pressure system meets a low-pressure system from the south. When the warm air is forced up into the atmosphere, it freezes and then dumps a lot of snow.)

Climatologists cannot say exactly how weather conditions will be affected in Minnesota as the warming continues. An increase in average temperature may cause more precipitation by producing low-pressure weather systems. Or the higher temperatures may increase the rate of evaporation from soils and cause drought. The outcome is still unclear, but a trend may be appearing. According to the Minnesota Pollution Control Agency, precipitation has already increased by about 20 percent, especially in the southern half of the state. Either scenario could have significant implications for the state's ecosystems, as well as for the economy and the health and safety of its citizens:

- Drier soils would cause the decline of forests. The forests would be replaced by prairies or, more likely, by grassland and pasture used to feed cattle. Evaporation would also result in lower water levels—a concern even for a region known as the Land of Ten Thousand Lakes. This situation might be made worse by the need to divert extra water for crop irrigation. Alternatively, drought-resistant crops may have to replace those currently being grown. (Some crops, such as wheat, thrive in dry climates and might benefit or be unaffected.)

- A warmer, wetter climate would stimulate the growth of forests. Crops might require less irrigation. However, the risk of flooding of the state's rivers and lakes would also increase.

Change Everywhere

Climate change in Minnesota may not mean much to people living in other parts of the United States or to citizens of other countries, but it is an indicator of things to come in many parts of the world. For example, Germany also has a continental climate. Temperatures there increased by as much as 1.8 °F (1 °C) during the twentieth century—a change almost identical to Minnesota's. Its forests, cropland, and cities are likely to respond similarly to global warming.

Florida can serve as an example of change in warmer climates or coastal climates. This state has deciduous and coniferous forest in the north; to the south, subtropical ecosystems host swamps, palm trees, mangrove forests, and coral reefs. Because of its shape and position, Florida also has a very extensive coastline and is therefore in the path of tropical storms. A study conducted by Tufts University in Medford, Massachusetts, in 2007 indicates that Florida may one day face a number of climate-related challenges, including

- increased costs of electricity generation as temperatures and air-conditioning requirements rise

- increased hurricane damage

- reduced real estate values from sea-level rise

- loss of tourism revenue as a result of unappealing changes in the landscape

Scientists have still not reached agreement about how global warming affects tropical storms and hurricanes. (Hurricanes are also known as cyclones and typhoons, depending on the ocean in which they form.) In 2008 separate studies were released with conflicting opinions. Scientists at the National Oceanic and Atmospheric Administration (NOAA) think that the overall number of storms in the Atlantic could decline by 2060, mostly due to wind shear. Wind shear occurs when winds rapidly change direction and speed at the top of clouds; this disruption can stop tropical storm clouds from building into hurricanes. A second study, from Florida State University, found that hurricanes will grow stronger in response to warmer ocean temperatures. More studies and time will be needed to resolve this disparity. For now, the only certainty is that ocean water has warmed by approximately 0.5 °F (0.28 °C).

Scientists do agree that global warming produces a rise in sea level (though they quibble about the exact amount). Melting polar ice, which contributes to some of this rise in water levels, is caused by increasing air and water temperature. Thermal expansion also affects sea level. When the thermal energy of a substance increases, its particles move faster and spread out. The volume of the substance increases. Water in a container (such as an ocean basin) has

Warming ocean waters may continue to generate hurricanes. In this satellite image, Hurricane Dean heads toward Mexico's Yucatán Peninsula in August 2007.

only one place to go as it expands: up. The Intergovernmental Panel on Climate Change (IPCC) reports on the effects of ocean warming:

> Observations since 1961 show that the average temperature of the global ocean has increased to depths of at least 3000 m and that the ocean has been absorbing more than 80% of the heat added to the climate system.

Melting ice and thermal expansion combined to produce an average sea level rise of 0.07 inches (1.8 millimeters) per year from 1961 to 2003. The total rise equals almost 3 inches (7.5 centimeters).

Hurricane Season Blows In

The year 2005 brought fifteen hurricanes—more than any year on record—including Katrina, Rita, and Wilma, all of which at one stage were category 5 storms (with winds above 155 miles per hour [mph], or 249 kilometers per hour [kph]). Katrina will go down in history for its damage to the Gulf Coast and to New Orleans. Wilma made the record books as the most intense Atlantic storm of all time, based on the low barometric pressure within its eye.

For the 2008 hurricane season, meteorologists predicted the development of thirteen named tropical storms in the Atlantic. They believed that seven of these would become hurricanes, with three storms at category 3 or above (winds of at least 111 mph, or 178 kph). In early spring meteorologists revised their forecast, recognizing the signs of an unusual number of storms in the season to come. In 2008 Tropical Storm Arthur got the season off to an early start by emerging near Belize, in Central America, on May 30. By early September ten storms had been named. Five of these—Bertha, Dolly, Gustav, Hanna, and Ike—became hurricanes. On a single day, September 2, four storms in different stages swirled in different regions of the Atlantic. Gustav reached category 4 status as it struck Cuba but weakened before reaching New Orleans. As it wound down, Ike gained force, sweeping through the Gulf Coast region as Hanna wreaked havoc in the Caribbean. The season ended in mid–November after causing more than 850 deaths and $41 billion in damages.

Earth's Changing Climate

In 2008 most of the city of Venice, Italy—including its historic St. Mark's Square—experienced record flooding that has been attributed to global warming.

Clearly, life on Earth is changing. Some regions already see radical differences; in others, climate change may be barely noticeable for many years to come. Learning about the forces that influence climate change will increase the possibility of reducing its negative effects.

Why the Fuss?

Periodic episodes of global warming and cooling have been a regular part of Earth's 4.54-billion-year history. So why is climate change such a big deal now? The answer is simple: it will change life on Earth dramatically. In its 2007 report the IPCC stated:

Human beings are exposed to climate change through changing weather patterns (for example, more intense and frequent extreme events) and indirectly through changes in water, air, food quality and quantity, ecosystems, agriculture, and economy. At this early stage the effects are small but are projected to progressively increase in all countries and regions.

The U.S. Environmental Protection Agency (EPA) further explains how global warming and climate change can impact human health:

Throughout the world, the prevalence of some diseases and other threats to human health depend largely on local climate. Extreme temperatures can lead directly to loss of life, while climate-related disturbances in ecological systems, such as changes in the range of infective parasites, can indirectly impact the incidence of serious infectious diseases. In addition, warm temperatures can increase air and water pollution, which in turn harm human health.

Conditions that can cause climate change are called forcings, and they may be external or internal (relative to Earth). There are two types of external forcings: changes to the amount of light produced by the Sun and regular cycles that alter Earth's motion. In the past, internal forcings have been produced by large-scale natural events such as volcanic eruptions, huge continental plate motions, and ocean circulation. These and other internal forcings can shift the balance of greenhouse gases in the atmosphere. Greenhouse gases—primarily water vapor, carbon dioxide, methane, nitrous oxide, tropospheric ozone, and fluorinated gases—function like the glass walls and ceiling of a greenhouse. They allow ultraviolet radiation (light) to pass down through the atmosphere but absorb infrared radiation (heat) given off by the planet. Some of this heat is released into the atmosphere, but a significant amount is reradiated to Earth's surface. As the concentrations of greenhouse gases change, so does the planet's temperature.

Earth's Changing Climate

The burning of fossil fuels has contributed to the amount of greenhouse gases in the atmosphere.

Humans are now considered a source of internal forcing. The use of fossil fuels, alteration of the landscape, disposal of waste, and production of chemicals have contributed greenhouse gases to the atmosphere. The planet is warming as a result, just as it always has when greenhouse gas levels have been high from natural forcings. Although there are substantial records of Earth's past climate, there is only one known episode during which greenhouse gases rose so quickly. As a result, scientists cannot effectively predict how Earth's many systems will respond to the rising temperature or its effects on the growing human population.

Mr. Gore's Truth

Former vice president Al Gore first learned about global warming as a college student while taking a class with Dr. Roger Revelle at Harvard University. In the 1950s Revelle had begun studying the role of carbon dioxide (CO_2) in Earth's atmosphere. He and his colleagues found that

Former vice president Al Gore has taken a great interest in the topic of global warming. Here he speaks at the Climate Project Conference in Mexico City in 2009.

the oceans can absorb large amounts of CO_2. In a paper on the subject, they wrote that "most of the CO_2 released by artificial fuel combustion since the beginning of the industrial revolution must have been absorbed by the oceans." In other words, humans had not yet noticed the true impact of CO_2 emissions on the atmosphere because the oceans (rather than the atmosphere) were absorbing a large percentage of the emissions.

At the end of that decade, instruments were installed atop Mauna Loa, a high volcano on the island of Hawaii. The location was chosen because it was accessible to scientists but also very high in the atmosphere and far from sources of human pollution. These instruments would provide samples of carbon dioxide that could represent the gas's concentration in the global atmosphere. A climate scientist named Charles Keeling was in charge of the project. In May 1958 Keeling

The Keeling Curve

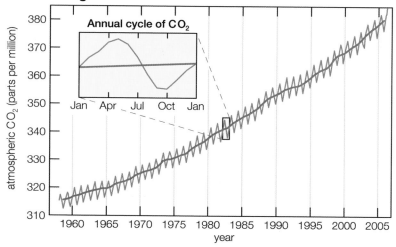

Continuous measurements of CO_2 concentration in Earth's atmosphere show a steady increase since the study began in the 1950s.

obtained CO_2 readings of approximately 314 parts per million (ppm)—314 CO_2 molecules for every million total molecules of air. Inexplicably, the level dropped over the summer and then began to rise again in the spring. In March 1959 the reading was 315 ppm. Over a period of years, Keeling collected data showing the regular annual fluctuations of carbon dioxide concentrations. The saw-edged graph of this data is named after him; it is called the Keeling Curve. Monitoring of CO_2 levels has continued on Mauna Loa and in May 2009 showed a concentration of 386.93 ppm.

When he was elected to the U.S. House of Representatives in 1976, Gore began talking to his colleagues about the issue of global warming. In 2000, after completing two terms as vice president, he decided to give the issue his full attention. His 2006 movie, *An Inconvenient Truth*, laid out the data that reveal climate change around the world. In 2007 he and the IPCC were jointly awarded the Nobel Peace Prize "for their efforts to build up and disseminate greater knowledge about man-made climate change, and to lay the foundations for the measures that are needed to counteract such change."

Gore has not been the only American calling for legislation and action to reduce global warming, but he has certainly been the most famous. In the book *An Inconvenient Truth*, he writes:

> Nature . . . is slow-moving, undemanding, maybe underwhelming for many people. . . . But what we do to nature we do to ourselves. The magnitude of environmental destruction is now on a scale few ever foresaw; the wounds no longer simply heal themselves. We have to act affirmatively to stop the harm.

Two
Lessons from the Ancient Earth

As temperatures continue to rise and climates change around the globe, it is difficult to know how Earth will look or function in the centuries to come. Some clues may be found in the planet's ancient history.

The planets in Earth's solar system formed at the same time the Sun did. Earth was very hot in the early stages of this process, but this heat gradually dissipated as the fast-moving ball of gases, dust, and rocks eventually settled to form continents and oceans. Because the Sun was still young, it did not give off as much ultraviolet radiation (light) as today. The weak Sun could have left Earth cold and lifeless. This outcome was averted thanks to high concentrations of greenhouse gases (such as water vapor, carbon dioxide, and methane) in the atmosphere, which reradiated Earth's own heat; this process slowly warmed the planet.

The young planet experienced long periods of rain. As water vapor condenses into rain, it reacts with carbon dioxide in the atmosphere and produces carbonic acid, a weak acidic solution. Over long periods, this acid rain can erode rock. The loose sediment from the rock accumulates on land and in the sea and gradually forms new layers of rock, in which the carbon is locked for millions of years. By 2.3 billion years ago, the levels of carbon dioxide had fallen so low that the greenhouse effect was drastically reduced. As a result, Earth entered its first glacial period, which may have lasted for millions of years.

Approximately 750 million years ago, Earth entered a second major glacial phase. This glaciation may have occurred because microscopic organisms called cyanobacteria had moved onto land and began to weather the rocks. As they did so, carbon dioxide was removed from the environment. Another influence may have been the rapid shifting of continents, which also erodes rocks and reduces carbon levels. Either way, glaciers spread from both poles to near the equator. Global average temperatures may have declined to –58 °F (–50 °C). Two theories explain how the planet warmed from this "snowball" condition. According to one theory, active volcanoes spewed ash and gases into the atmosphere, even during the height of glaciation. The gradual addition of carbon dioxide enhanced the greenhouse effect, melting the ice and warming the planet far above today's temperatures. A second hypothesis suggests that carbon dioxide stored in ocean water may have been circulated into the atmosphere by the addition of oxygen from the ice. A repetition of this freeze-and-thaw cycle continued for about 170 million years; as many as four major climate shifts took place before Earth finally settled to a more moderate temperature.

A rare exception to this glacial trend was a long warming period that began during the Cretaceous Period, approximately 144 million years ago. This period may have been the warmest since Earth finished its initial formation. In 2009 the global average temperature was approximately 58.5 °F (14.7 °C). During parts of the Cretaceous, average global temperatures were 10 to 20 °F (5.5–11.1 °C) higher. This difference may not seem tremendous, but in fact almost the entire planet had a tropical climate—even the poles. The trigger for this dramatic warming was a rise in greenhouse gas levels, a rise spurred by volcanic activity that lasted for tens

Feedbacks on Ice

Every system experiences inputs (external forces that have the potential to cause change). The system may respond in a way that offsets the input and reduces change. This result is called a negative feedback. Positive feedback occurs when the system changes along with the input.

An important example of positive feedback is albedo, the brightness of an object, which determines its ability to reflect sunlight. Ice has a high albedo—it can reflect much of the sunlight that strikes its surface. This characteristic allows the ice to stay cool and may even decrease the temperature of surrounding water or air enough to allow more ice to form. Albedo is a positive feedback mechanism that maintains the depth and extent of ice in Earth's polar regions. The effect is enhanced during glacial periods, when global temperatures fall.

Positive feedback also occurs when air and water temperatures warm around the ice. Ice extent is reduced, and dark meltwater ponds and cracks appear on the surface of the remaining blocks. The exposed land and water have a lower albedo. Thus, sunlight is absorbed rather than reflected and so the temperature near the surface increases, as does the rate of melting.

Climate scientists debate whether clouds act as a negative or positive feedback mechanism in this melting scenario. Clouds form as water evaporates from the warming Earth. These clouds provide a negative feedback mechanism by blocking some of the sunlight streaming onto Earth's surface and thus reducing temperature slightly. However, clouds can also absorb heat that is reflected upward from Earth's surface. This phenomenon is another positive feedback that leads to melting.

A warming trend during the Cretaceous Period led to a tropical environment on Earth.

of thousands of years. This volcanic period must have been truly spectacular.

Volcanoes emit a variety of materials that cause conflicting effects in the environment:

- Gases such as sulfur dioxide can cause smog at ground level, as they currently do near Hawaii's most active volcano, Kilauea.

- Ash and gases that spread into the atmosphere after a single massive eruption may reflect sunlight and reduce global temperature for some period. The eruption of Indonesia's Mount Tambora in 1815 was the largest volcanic eruption in recorded history. The year after its eruption was known as "the year without summer." Crops failed in Europe and North America, sea and glacier ice expanded, and thousands of people died.

- Volcanoes also emit greenhouse gases. Much of the carbon dioxide is absorbed into the oceans, where microscopic organisms such as corals use it to make calcium carbonate—the hard material of their shells.

Fossil records suggest that in the Cretaceous, carbon dioxide concentrations were so high that the oceans became unable to absorb the gas. A mass extinction of ocean organisms took place 93 million years ago, probably in response to the oxygen shortage that resulted from excess CO_2.

The Pleistocene ice ages began approximately 2 million years ago. This glaciation was more extensive in the Northern Hemisphere (the half of the planet north of the equator), though it also increased the mass of ice already formed on the continent of Antarctica. Many theories have been proposed for the glaciation's origin. Dust created by the rapid rise of the Tibetan Plateau (an enormous complex of mountain ranges in central Asia) may have built up in the atmosphere and blocked sunlight. A change in ocean currents could also have sped up the rate of evaporation from the oceans and increased rainfall over Europe and Asia. Rainwater runoff from the northern parts of these regions enters the Arctic Ocean. The additional fresh water may have lowered both temperature and salinity (concentration of salts). It would have been easier for ice to accumulate in these conditions, because fresh water has a higher freezing point than salt water.

The most recent period of the Pleistocene is called the Wisconsinan glaciation. At its height, 20,000 years ago, ice extended from the North Pole as far south as 45 degrees north latitude (the latitude of Minneapolis). Ice blanketed as much as 32 percent of the planet, including much of the United States, Canada, and Europe, as well as a large section of Russia. Where Chicago now sits, a sheet of ice 1 mile (1.6 km) thick covered the landscape. Sea level was at least 394 feet (120 meters) lower due to the mass of ice that was drawn up into glaciers.

This map illustrates the ice sheet range in the Northern Hemisphere during the Pleistocene.

Milankovitch's Cycles

In the 1920s a mathematician named Milutin Milankovitch figured out that glacial cycles are influenced by three aspects of Earth's motion: eccentricity, tilt, and precession. These aspects determine solar insolation—the amount of solar energy that is received on a given area of Earth's surface. In general, insolation is greatest for regions directly facing the Sun at any time of the year and those closest to the equator.

Most students learn in elementary school that Earth orbits the Sun. This orbit is not quite circular; it is slightly flattened to form an ellipse. The Sun is slightly off center rather than in the middle of this orbit. Perihelion is the point where Earth's orbit takes it closest to the Sun. Aphelion is the point where Earth's orbit takes it farthest from the Sun. On this orbital path, Earth sometimes passes nearby planets, which exert a gravitational pull that elongates Earth's orbit. (Imagine stretching a rubber band very gently.) When the planets move apart over time, Earth's orbit "rebounds" to a rounder shape. Changes in the shape of Earth's orbit are called eccentricity. When Earth is farther from the Sun, at aphelion, the ellipse is most flattened. At these times, insolation is exceptionally low. This low insolation promotes a glacial period. Milankovitch said that this cycle of stretching

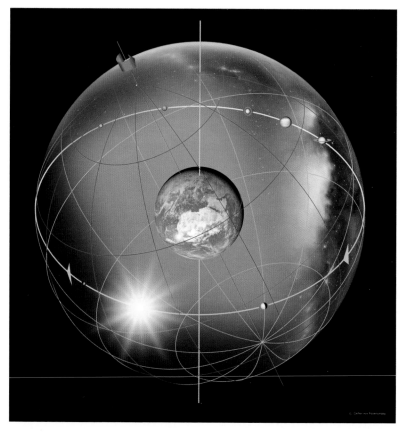

Computer artwork illustrates Earth's rotation and the movement of the Sun and planets in relation to it.

and rebounding takes 100,000 years; so glacial periods should also begin about that often.

Earth's orbit may become longer, but it always moves on the same plane relative to the Sun. Earth's poles are not pointed at a 90-degree angle to this plane but are tilted. This tilt is currently 23.5 degrees. When the Northern Hemisphere is oriented directly toward the Sun, summer occurs; in the Southern Hemisphere, it is winter because that part of the Earth faces away from the Sun. Earth has about a 3-degree range in its tilt, from about 21 to 24 degrees. As the planet tilts away from the Sun, insolation is reduced and glaciers may grow. Tilting toward the Sun increases the planet's temperature. It takes about 41,000 years for the planet to gradually tilt up on its axis and then tip down and back again.

Finally, Milankovitch looked at the precession of Earth's axis. This phenomenon is sometimes compared to the motion of a top that is beginning to slow down: the axis does not remain in one place but moves in a small circle. It takes Earth's axis almost 26,000 years to complete the path. This turning motion causes the hemispheres to switch places relative to the Sun. The impact on seasons is dramatic. For example, the Northern Hemisphere currently experiences summer when Earth is at aphelion—the point farthest from the Sun. The Southern Hemisphere summer takes place when the planet is at perihelion. The Southern Hemisphere therefore experiences much hotter summers. Precession will gradually turn the Northern Hemisphere to face the Sun at perihelion.

Proxy Evidence

Since the mid–1800s, Earth's temperature has been measured directly using equipment such as thermometers and, more recently, satellites. There are no such records of past climates, however. As a result, Milankovitch's theory of glacial cycles was considered purely theoretical until the mid–1960s. At that time Wallace Broecker, a professor and scientist at Columbia University in New York City, began to examine a group of fossil coral reefs near the Caribbean island of Barbados. The sea level falls during a widespread

A curator at the National Ice Core Lab in Littleton, Colorado, inspects an ice sample from Antarctica's Lake Vostok, which helps scientists reconstruct Earth's climates.

glacial event because water is pulled up and frozen into ice. Corals stop growing in the ice. Researchers were able to match the dates of coral fossils to glacial events. The oldest fossils were 122,000 years old, a length of time that corresponds to the beginning of the last major ice age. The reefs showed distinct patterns of growth and die-offs after that time in patterns matching the cycles for tilt and precession. Ice cores taken from Vostok Station, near the South Pole in Antarctica, confirm this pattern. Brian Fagan, an archaeologist, explains it this way:

> The Vostok ice core takes us to about 420,000 years ago, through four transitions from glacial to warm periods. . . . There seem to be two periodicities involved, a primary one of about 100,000 years and another, weaker one of about 41,000 years. Together,

they support the long-held theory that changes in the orbital parameters of the earth—eccentricity, [tilt], and precession of axis—cause variations in the intensity and distribution of solar radiation. These in turn trigger natural climatic changes on a grand scale.

Fossils and ice cores are called proxy records—they provide evidence of past climates, which cannot be measured directly. Other proxy records include tree rings and the sediments from ocean and lake bottoms. Each of these records gives different clues about environmental conditions in the past: temperature, precipitation, gases, types and levels of particles in the atmosphere (such as pollen, dust, or volcanic ash), as well as the diversity of organisms present. Human cultures, past and present, also provide proxy records. Some have kept written records; others have revealed information through their clothing or art. All records reveal that climate change has wrought both dramatic and exciting change on Earth.

Three

Life in the Holocene

As the Wisconsinan ice sheets began to withdraw about 12,000 years ago, Earth entered the most recent of many interglacial periods—the "breaks" between ice ages. These periods occur after every 100,000-year cycle and may last 8,000 to 40,000 years. The current interglacial has been named the Holocene. Interglacials are marked by increases in greenhouse gases. The Vostok cores show that carbon dioxide levels dip as low as 180 parts per million (ppm) during glacial periods and may rise to 300 ppm during interglacials.

According to ice core data, the interglacial began with a dramatic event: a temperature spike of 15 °F (8.3 °C) that took place in just ten years. This kind of global warming is very rare in the known proxy records but shows that Earth's climate can change very rapidly. Temperature has gradually increased over the intervening 10,000 years. Antarctic ice cores also confirm that greenhouse gases—especially carbon dioxide, nitrous oxide, and methane—have been closely related to temperature during all glacial and interglacial periods of the past 650,000 years. The several unusually warm or cold periods known during the Holocene show that greenhouse gases may fluctuate in response to external or internal forcings.

Humans and Climate

Climate may not be entirely responsible for human culture, but it has always had a great influence on lifestyles. People first began to settle down as farmers 12,000 years ago, just as the last ice age was in decline. Rather than hunting and herding animals across large areas and gathering other foods from the landscape, they settled where water resources were reliable and food could be grown and stored to support them year-round.

People in ancient Mesopotamia, an area also referred to as the Fertile Crescent, relied on weather patterns for their highly agricultural way of life.

The region where agriculture began—the Fertile Crescent (largely in present-day Turkey and Iraq)—is home to two of the world's great rivers: the Tigris and the Euphrates. They flow from the mountainous regions of Turkey through the lowland plains that now form Syria and Iraq and finally drain into the Persian Gulf. Despite the presence of these great rivers, rainfall was unpredictable, and ancient people dealt with regular droughts. As the region's population increased, competition for resources—including food and water—became serious. Brian Fagan explains how these problems were overcome:

> In more crowded landscapes, where people had already cultivated the landscape where wild plants once grew, hunger and death were inevitable. . . . Farmers came to depend on river floods and rregular rainfall, on irrigation systems that brought life-giving water to otherwise uncultivable land. The Mesopotamian solution was the city, located close to strategic irrigation canals that drew water from the Tigris or Euphrates rivers.

Early Mesopotamian communities built walls to protect their resources. The first human cities arose within. One of the greatest was Uruk. By 3200 BCE, Uruk had an early form of government, sophisticated architecture and art, and even an early form of writing.

Beginning in 900 CE and continuing for a period of about four hundred years, the Northern Hemisphere experienced slightly warmer temperatures than average. This period is known as the Medieval Warm Period. For Europeans, the temperature increase was just enough to improve crop growth. Gentler winters encouraged Norse settlers on Iceland to venture on toward Greenland. In regions closer to the equator, the effects were not so beneficial. Anasazi Indians in what is now the southwestern United States may have been driven from their desert homes by drought. The great Mayan civilization, located on Mexico's Yucatán Peninsula, once supported at least 8 million people. It collapsed after a series of three intense droughts early in the Warm Period.

Earth's Changing Climate

The four-hundred-year warming trend, the Medieval Warm Period, allowed the Norse to explore and settle Greenland.

As the Medieval Warm Period drew to a close, it was immediately followed by a shift toward much cooler conditions. The Little Ice Age began around 1300 and lasted until 1850. Ice cores from Greenland show that winters during the first century of the Little Ice Age were colder than any in seven hundred years. Written records from Europe and Asia reveal that these centuries were prone to rapid, sometimes yearly swings in temperature and precipitation—alternately rainy and dry, alternately snowy or frigidly cold and warm. Crops suffered from the variation, and in many years people went hungry.

One suggested cause of this variable climate was a series of reductions in solar irradiance (the amount of solar energy produced), which occurred at the same time as the Little Ice Age. Solar irradiance fluctuates in a cycle that lasts eleven years, with a high point of irradiance (maximum) and a low point (minimum). This cycle is influenced by the number of sunspots, which are regions of low temperature on the surface of the Sun. In fact, regions of higher magnetic activity surround

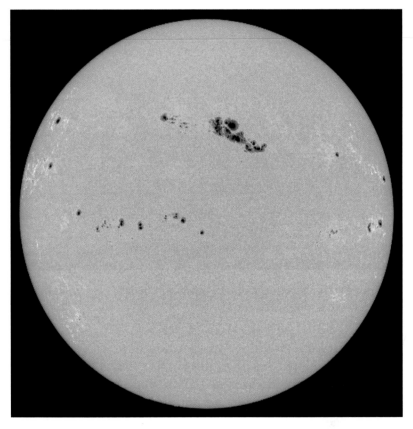

When sunspot activity (dark areas on Sun above) rises, Earth experiences an increase in solar irradiance.

them; this activity increases the brightness of the Sun and the amount of radiation it emits. When sunspot activity declines (during the minimum), Earth receives less solar energy and therefore experiences some degree of global cooling.

A significant outcome of the Little Ice Age was the increase in the use of coal in England. By this time, coal had been burned as a fuel in China for almost 1,400 years. People in the Bronze Age (2100–750 BCE) discovered coal in the British Isles, and Romans made use of it during their occupation of the isles (43–410 CE). The use of coal did not catch on among

A French iron foundry burns coal to operate its machinery during the Industrial Revolution.

Britons until the twelfth century, when mining began in earnest near the North Sea. Burning of this soft coal created acrid fumes, which drifted through the air and irritated the lungs of anyone nearby. The smoke polluted homes and skylines. In 1306 King Edward I passed what may be the first environmental law in history; it outlawed the use of coal. However, Britain's population was growing and their traditional source of fuel—wood from forestlands—began to shrink from overharvesting. Coal provided a cheap replacement to fuel fires during the long, cold winters, and so the law was ignored.

Eighteenth-century British engineers began to design coal-powered steam engines. Ironically, these engines were first used to pump water into coal mines, increasing the rate at which coal could be extracted. Soon the steam engine was modified to run factory machines, train locomotives, ships, and other devices. Manufacturing and transportation underwent radical transformations: materials once made by hand could now be produced in mass quantities, while people and goods could travel much faster over long distances. The Industrial Revolution had begun.

The past 150 years have brought remarkable changes in climate. In 2007 scientists from the IPCC stated,

> The late 20th century has been unusually warm. Palaeoclimatic reconstructions show that the second half of the 20th century was likely the warmest 50-year period in the Northern Hemisphere in the last 1300 years. This rapid warming is consistent with the scientific understanding of how the climate should respond to a rapid increase in greenhouse gases like that which has occurred over the past century, and the warming is inconsistent with the scientific understanding of how the climate should respond to natural external factors such as variability in solar output and volcanic activity.

It has taken decades for scientists and citizens to accept that humans have played a role in climate change. Some people still believe that natural phenomena are responsible. Scientific evidence from many sources refute this idea.

- The Milankovitch cycles have proved to be consistent across long time frames. They place Earth in an interglacial period. Studies also show that CO_2 concentrations fluctuate regularly through these cycles, and temperature follows CO_2 levels. Yet CO_2 levels now exceed those in the long historical record. Some input aside from the Milankovitch cycles must be involved.

- Volcanoes can emit significant amounts of CO_2. However, consistent and widespread volcanic activity is required to increase global temperature. This level of volcanism has not occurred on Earth in millennia. The eruption of Mount Agung on Bali, in the Pacific Ocean, was the largest volcanic eruption in the twentieth century. As in the case of Mount Tambora, Agung emitted just enough gases

and particles to act as a shield in the atmosphere. The eruption is believed to have lowered temperatures by several tenths of a degree for about a year.

- Earth is currently at a minimum in the solar irradiance cycle. (The maximum will occur in 2012.) However, there are some impacts from solar irradiance. In 2004 NASA scientists calculated that global temperature fluctuates by 0.18 °F (0.1 °C) during the solar irradiance cycle. This fluctuation would have contributed to some warming during maximum points in past cycles. The sun has also become slightly more active since the Little Ice Age and thus has a slightly larger impact overall. As a result, solar irradiance can account for about 25 percent of the warming that has occurred during the past century.

In other words, forcings that have historically led to climate change cannot fully explain the global warming that is now under way.

Four

The Ice Breaks

John Cabot was a man with a mission. Born in the early 1450s, Cabot became a spice merchant whose work took him around the Mediterranean. Many of his colleagues and competitors sailed as far as Asia in search of valuable spices and other goods that would make them wealthy. Italian traders took a route leading eastward from the Red Sea into the Indian and Pacific oceans. The Portuguese reached the same destinations by sailing around the African continent. Cabot knew that these journeys were long and fraught with dangers. He became convinced that a shorter route between Europe and Asia could be found and believed that it must lie to the northwest, across the Arctic and Pacific oceans.

The search for such a route began to consume Cabot's mind—but he needed money to begin. When Italian merchants turned him down, Cabot picked up his family and moved to Portugal and then to England. In 1496 Cabot met a group of merchants who offered to buy him a ship and provisions. Approval was also required from King Henry VII, who willingly granted it. Two years earlier, Pope Alexander VI had

split the known world into two halves; Portugal was given control over the eastern half and Spain the western. England was blocked from all trade routes. The king hoped that if Cabot found a new route, now being called the Northwest Passage, this discovery would allow England to rejoin the profitable trade in spices and other Asian goods.

In 1497, on his second attempt, Cabot located what he believed to be an island off the coast of Asia. Thanks to this apparent success, he was allowed to take a fleet of five vessels the next year. Cabot was shipwrecked on that journey, possibly on the northeastern shoreline of present-day Newfoundland—the same "island" he had discovered. Later explorers learned that Newfoundland was not an island but a large headland that reaches into the North Atlantic Ocean. Far from Asia, it is one of the northeasternmost points of land in North America.

Franklin's Fate

Finding the Northwest Passage became one of the great challenges of history. Explorers found that traversing the passage, if it existed, would require navigating through a maze of rugged islands just south of the Arctic Ocean. Here, floating blocks of ice filled the sea and threatened to trap ships in almost every month of the year. Those who attempted the feat suffered extreme cold, wind, isolation, and the long darkness of Arctic winters. Yet the expeditions continued. Almost 350 years after Cabot's death, the British Royal Navy informed Sir John Franklin that he would lead the latest attempt. Franklin was given two warships, *Terror* and *Erebus*. Iron plates were welded to their hulls to reduce the risk of punctures and provide more force while pushing through thick ice. Propellers—only recently invented—were installed to give additional thrust. These ships were fueled by coal-powered steam engines, also a new technology of the budding Industrial Revolution.

In 1845 Franklin set forth with more than 128 men and a bounty of provisions. The record shows that they stopped in Greenland. Soon after, they passed a whaling ship north of Baffin Bay, near the entrance to the passage. Then the

Italian navigator John Cabot reaches the shore of Newfoundland.

Earth's Changing Climate

Terror and *Erebus* seemed to vanish. It was many years before any evidence was found to explain their disappearance. That first autumn, Franklin chose to spend the winter on Beechey Island, west of Baffin Bay. Arctic waters hold pack ice through much of the year, but its extent is greater in winter, as the cold temperatures cause new ice to form and old ice to thicken. The ships set off again as the ice began to melt in the spring of 1846. Under normal circumstances, the ice would have continued to clear during the summer months. As they made their way between islands in the Canadian Arctic, however, the ships apparently encountered a labyrinth of thick ice. Franklin was forced to dock again, this time on the west side of King William Island. The crew lived in that spot for almost two years. Franklin died during this time. In April 1848 the remaining men made a desperate decision to walk away from the ships. Weakened by scurvy (deficiency of vitamin C) and frostbite, they also suffered from lead poisoning, which came from the solder used to seal their metal food cans. Some may have resorted to cannibalism in a last effort to survive. None of the members of the Franklin expedition ever made it off King William Island, however.

Thick ice hampered John Franklin's attempt to discover the Northwest Passage.

Captain Roald Amundsen was the first explorer to navigate the Northwest Passage in its entirety.

Half a century later, in 1903, a thirty-year-old sailor named Roald Amundsen set forth from Oslo, Norway, in a 72-foot (21-m) herring boat. After leaving Baffin Bay, he and his crew navigated around the Arctic islands, following a route very similar to that used by the Franklin expedition. As the summer drew to a close and conditions grew more dangerous, Amundsen agreed to turn into an uncharted strait along the eastern side of King William Island. The waters were treacherously shallow but clear enough of ice for the little boat to pass. The crew spent two years on the island, collecting scientific data and becoming familiar with the local Eskimo culture and people. In August 1905 the crew packed up and resumed the westward journey. Eventually they passed the shores where Franklin and his crew had perished. Days later, a crew member called out words that sent a rush of excitement into Amundsen's heart: "Vessel in sight!" It was another ship coming from San Francisco, a port in the Pacific Ocean to the southwest. It took another year to reach his final destination of Nome, Alaska, but Amundsen had already accomplished the most difficult part of the journey. He was the first to navigate the entire Northwest Passage.

Clues in the Ice

Pack ice forms when seawater reaches its freezing point (29 °F [–2 °C]). Thin, new ice is called seasonal ice. It may melt as air and water temperatures warm in the spring and summer. If it does not melt, pack ice grows thicker over a period of years. Thick, older ice is called perennial ice. More of the Arctic Ocean is covered by ice in March than at any other time of the year because both seasonal and perennial ice are present. By September the ice is at a minimum. Vessels may pass through the broken ice and slushy water.

As the Arctic Ocean warms, vessels are able to pass through the melting ice.

In contrast to pack ice, ice sheets and ice caps may last for hundreds of thousands of years. If air temperatures remain moderate, layers of ice will eventually build into large glaciers. There are two main categories. Constrained glaciers are limited in size by the landscape. They are typically located on mountain slopes or in valleys. These glaciers move slowly downhill under the force of gravity. Some flow onto flatter land; others end at the shoreline, where they may calve (lose) icebergs into the water. Unconstrained glaciers are also known as ice caps and ice sheets and may be very large. Currently, glaciers cover 10 percent of all land surface and hold approximately 75 percent of the planet's supply of fresh water.

A glacier's ice is a record of history. The characteristics of each layer—color, chemical composition, thickness, and more—provide information about environmental conditions of the past. Researchers can access this record by taking an ice core. In this procedure a hollow metal tube or drill is pushed down into the ice. A long, thin section of ice is trapped within and pulled up. As it is pulled up, the core is cut into small pieces that can be closely examined. Some cores reach down thousands of feet and include ancient layers of accumulated ice. Sections of the ice sheet on Greenland, a massive island on the eastern edge of the Arctic, are 2 miles (3.2 km) thick. The ice sheet's lowest layers are more than 110,000 years old. At a location called Dome C in Antarctica, the European Project for Ice Coring in Antarctica (EPICA) drilled a 2-mile (3.2-km) ice core that includes 800,000 years of ice.

Historians have long wondered why Sir John Franklin and his crew spent two summers on King William Island and never tried to escape. They should have been able to sail out when the ice was at its summer minimum. Polar researchers examined an ice core taken from the Arctic to see whether the climate had played any role. In most summers a thin layer of ice melts on the surface of a glacier. When it refreezes in winter, it creates a layer of clear ice. These clear layers alternate with opaque layers produced by winter snowpack. The Arctic core showed a five-year period in the 1840s with no clear layers. Here was the answer. Franklin had unknowingly

A scientist takes ice core samples from Canada's Yukon Territory to measure ancient carbon dioxide levels.

attempted to locate the Northwest Passage during an episode of exceptional cold, when the pack ice never melted—even in summer. By the time Amundsen made the trip, conditions had returned to normal. Temperatures were warm enough for him to sail during the warmer months, and he made it through the Northwest Passage in three years.

Changes in the Arctic

If Franklin and Amundsen could visit the Arctic today, they might find it hard to recognize the landscape and sea they fought so hard to cross. No one knows how thick the pack ice was in their time. The first measurements, taken by submarine in 1958, showed that perennial ice layers averaged 10 feet (3 m) in thickness. In 1974 NASA obtained a measurement of 9 feet (2.7 m). By 2005 satellite data indicated that pack ice was 40 percent thinner than in 1958, averaging only 6 feet (1.8 m).

Not only has ice become thinner on the Arctic Ocean, there is also less ice covering the surface of the water than a century ago. Scientists at the National Snow and Ice Data Center (NSIDC) in Colorado began their research by calculating the average extent of summer ice between 1979 (when satellite measurements began) and 2000. They obtained an average of 2.7 million square miles (7 million km²). This average is half the Arctic Ocean's total area of 5.4 million square miles (14 million km²), and at first it seems like an impressive number. However, when scientists look at the year-to-year data rather than the average, another story is revealed. It turns out that summer ice in the Arctic Ocean has declined steadily over that twenty-one-year period, at a rate of approximately 10 percent per decade.

Recently the situation has worsened. Faster summer melting resulted in the loss of both seasonal and perennial ice, and winter freezing could not fully replace the losses. By September 2007 ice extent was down to 1.65 million square miles (4.28 million km²). That figure is 39 percent below the 1979–2000 average and may represent only half the ice that would have been present in 1950. The Northwest Passage has also shown

Lights in the Sky

On a night when the skies are clear, the Moon is the most prominent object in the sky. The black canopy of space is also peppered with the glimmer of planets and stars. However, an observer of the night sky may also notice tiny lights that fly straight paths across the sky. These lights are artificial satellites.

The Soviet Union (USSR) surprised the world in 1957 by launching the first artificial satellite, *Sputnik 1*. This gleaming metal sphere, only 23 inches (58 cm) in diameter, zoomed around the planet so fast that it made fifteen orbits per day. Though its primary goal was to show that the USSR was ahead of all other nations in the "space race," *Sputnik 1* also provided valuable information on the density of Earth's atmosphere. In the five decades since that historic launch, more than 4,500 satellites have been put into space. Hundreds may be up at any given time, flying on different orbital paths; they are used for purposes as diverse as the study of distant star systems, business and communications, navigation, military defense, and weather and climate analysis.

A number of online programs—commercial products such as GoogleEarth and Microsoft Virtual Earth, as well as the U.S. Geological Survey's TerraServer—make satellite images available to citizens. Love the ocean? You can use satellite images to "fly" over the long stretch of sand and waves at New Zealand's Muriwai Beach. Studying volcanoes? Check out the brown-and-white cone of Mount Kilimanjaro. Concerned about the loss of rainforests? Inspect recent images of the Amazon. Or simply get a new perspective on your own neighborhood.

This satellite image captures Arctic ice conditions at the end of the melt season in 2007, when sea ice extent was at a record low.

its vulnerability. Historically, in summer it has been filled with swirls of broken ice and patches of open water. On August 29, 2007, satellite images revealed very little ice. Instead, indigo blue water filled most of the passage. Late the next summer, the Northwest Passage opened once again. On the far side of the Arctic Ocean, another shipping passage, known as the Northern Sea Route, opened in early September. The National Oceanic and Atmospheric Administration's National Ice Center reported the event, noting, "This is the first recorded occurrence of the Northwest Passage and Northern Sea Route both being open at the same time." This simultaneous melting along the shorelines created a gigantic "island" of ice in the middle of the Arctic Ocean; theoretically, it would have been possible to navigate a ship all the way around its perimeter. Some scientists suggest that these conditions have not existed since before the last ice age began, 125,000 years ago.

Polar scientists have noticed declines in ice throughout the cryosphere, the regions of Earth that contain snow and ice for any part of the year. These regions include the Arctic and Antarctic, high mountain regions throughout the world, and much of the Northern Hemisphere in winter. International Polar Year (IPY) 2007–08—an extensive scientific research program organized under the auspices of the International Council for Science and the World Meteorological Organization—allowed thousands of scientists from more than sixty nations to share knowledge and resources while conducting more than two hundred different research projects over a two-year period. The IPY's goal statement explains some of the serious problems that result from global changes to snow and ice:

> Changes in the large ice sheets will impact global sea level, affecting coastal cities and low-lying areas. Changes in snowfall and shrinkage of glaciers will influence millions of people whose daily use of water for personal consumption or for agriculture depends on snowpack and glacial sources. Thermal degradation of permafrost will mobilize vast reserves of frozen carbon, some of which, as methane, will increase the global greenhouse effect. Changes in sea ice combined with enhanced river inputs of freshwater will lead to substantial changes in ocean circulation. Warming of polar oceans, coupled with changes in ice coverage and river run-off, will alter marine ecosystems with consequences for globally-significant fisheries.

The Demise of Larsen B

Earth observation satellites are ideal for studying the cryosphere. *Terra* and *Aqua* are used by many researchers in the United States; another is *Envisat*, launched in 2002 by the European Space Agency. *Envisat*, orbiting the planet at an altitude of about 500 miles (800 km), takes continuous photos and measurements of the planet's surface and atmosphere.

Measuring the Ice

Humans use microwaves for purposes such as cooking, radar, and radio transmissions. Radar (actually an acronym for *radio detection and ranging*) is a form of "active microwave" because the microwaves are intentionally emitted from a source. The waves that reflect off objects in the surrounding objects can be used for detection. Many objects on Earth emit passive microwaves as a result of their energy. All microwaves occur in a variety of wavelengths—measuring 0.4 inches to 11.8 inches (1 cm–30 cm). One factor that influences wavelength is the structure of the emitting object. For example, the water molecule has a different crystalline structure than ice. It produces passive microwaves of a slightly different wavelength. Soil has yet a different structure.

Passive microwaves are useful to scientists because their long wavelengths can penetrate the atmosphere. Earth-observation satellites (EOSs) are specifically designed to obtain information about Earth's surface and atmosphere. More than 150 EOSs currently orbit the planet. Some are mounted with sensors that can detect this radiation. The U.S. satellites *Terra* and *Aqua* run a program called the Moderate Resolution Imaging Spectroradiometer (MODIS), which converts passive microwaves to a high-resolution image of the landscape. Polar researchers can use MODIS's passive microwave data to compare the extent of ice to open water or land. Such images also make it possible to observe the daily changes in individual sections of ice or obtain a large-scale view of the cryosphere in order to track ice over time.

It has a fast orbit that covers the entire planet in thirty-five days, but it also passes over Earth's poles on each orbit.

At the time of *Envisat*'s launch, scientists were watching an ice shelf called Larsen B on the eastern side of the Antarctic Peninsula. This narrow arm of land reaches northward off the Antarctic continent into the Atlantic Ocean. An ice shelf is much like an ice sheet except that it extends from the land onto the surface of the ocean. Its leading edge (the front) is in the open water. Ice began to calve from the front of Larsen B in the 1990s, and researchers expected the 12,000-year-old shelf to collapse eventually. The main body of ice was still 720 feet (220 m) thick in places, however, so *Envisat*'s images on January 31, 2002, came as a shock. Larsen B's wide, crescent-shaped band of ice normally showed up glittering white. That day it was marked with horizontal blue lines stretching inward from the front. By March 7 most of the shelf—which was larger than Rhode Island—had shattered, cracked, and crumbled. More than 720 billion tons (653 billion tonnes [also called metric tons]) of ice were left afloat on the Weddell Sea. The remainder of the Larsen B ice shelf has continued to break away in bits and pieces since 2002.

Before its collapse, Larsen B acted like a dam and thus prevented several glaciers from adding ice to the ocean. Without the ice shelf to block their path, the lower edges of these glaciers began to flow faster. Glaciers move because of the force of gravity, but when they are very thick, the ice does not usually crack. Instead, the glacier deforms: the molecules slide past each other, and the ice moves like thick, melted plastic. Friction on the bottom surface often causes the top layers to flow faster. As a result, the rapidly moving glacier becomes thinner. Warm temperatures may also cause melting from the bottom. Like the microthin layer of melted ice under an ice skate, meltwater lubricates a glacier and speeds up its flow. The Hektoria Glacier had already been accelerating by 0.04 inches (1 mm) per day. After the collapse of Larsen B, it experienced a surge. The Hektoria's flow rate began to increase rapidly, adding 0.55 inches (14 mm) per day to its speed.

Floating and Melting

In physics the Archimedes' Principle is used to describe why objects float or sink. It can be useful when thinking about the effect of ice on sea level. Archimedes' Principle states that "the buoyant force on a submerged object is equal to the weight of the fluid that is displaced by the object."

There is an easy way to think of this situation. Every object has a certain volume. When an object is placed in a container of water, it takes up space—so the water level rises. Volume is not the only factor in play, however. A simple test will demonstrate the principle. Fill a large container with water. Carefully measure the height (level) of the water in the container. Take a bowling ball and drop it in the water. Measure the water level. Now do the same with a coconut. What happens? The bowling ball sinks, and the coconut floats; the ball also raises the water level higher because the ball weighs more than an equal volume of water. Cut the ball and the coconut in half, and try the test again. The result is comparable. The answer is straightforward: the density of an object—its mass per unit volume—determines how much water is displaced.

Ice is simply water that has frozen. However, water expands as it freezes, so ice is slightly less dense than water. Thus, ice shelves weighing billions of tons (tonnes) float atop the ocean. Icebergs created by Larsen B's collapse cannot affect sea level even if they melt because, according to Archimedes' Principle, their volume already increased sea level long ago, when the ice first entered the sea. New icebergs calved from glaciers do affect sea level, however, because they are added to the water.

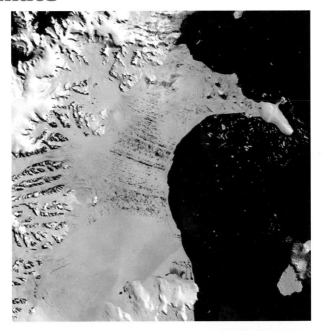

These two satellite images of the Larsen B ice shelf were taken on January 1, 2002 (top) and March 7, 2007 (bottom). By March 7 the ice shelf had collapsed.

Why did Larsen B collapse at all? Explaining such a complex event requires scientists to reconstruct the scene, much as detectives do after a crime. Typically, there are ultimate and proximate causes for such a large event. Ultimate causes build up over the long term, while proximate causes are the "last straws" that result in an event's final occurrence. Evidence strongly indicates that the ultimate cause of Larsen B's collapse was a subtle increase in air temperature that took place over many decades. Studies have shown that there is a threshold temperature for ice shelves to remain stable or grow. Antarctica's threshold is 23 °F (–5 °C). On the Antarctic Peninsula, however, temperatures have increased by 0.9 °F (0.5 °C) per decade since the 1940s.

At least three proximate causes have been suggested for Larsen B's collapse. Dr. Ted Scambos and his team from the NSIDC in Boulder, Colorado, believe that meltwater is responsible. According to Scambos's hypothesis, the length of the melt season (the spring, summer, and fall months, when it is too warm to freeze) determines how much water melts on the ice shelf's surface. Ice shelves are not perfectly solid; they contain air pockets that were present when the ice formed. When the melt season is long, a large amount of meltwater can trickle down and fill those pockets. Moving water can also melt through the ice, forming streams on the surface and deep crevasses that bore down into the shelf. Although some refreezing occurs in winter, a series of melting events over many years may weaken the shelf beyond recovery.

Scientists at the British Antarctic Survey concur that meltwater is the problem, but they blame the melting on unusually strong westerly winds over the Antarctic Peninsula. Since the 1960s the average summer temperature on the peninsula has been 36 °F (2.2 °C). Warm westerlies cause temperatures to rise by as much as 18 °F (12 °C)—a significant push that could increase the rate of melting. Dr. Douglas MacAyeal, from the University of Chicago, also believes that melting weakens the ice; but MacAyeal suggests a very different proximate cause of ice shelf collapse. Storms can create ocean swells that

One cause of the Larsen B collapse was due to meltwater on the ice shelf. Meltwater glacial streams such as this weaken ice shelves.

travel long distances across the surface of the ocean. Although these swells may be too small for ships to notice, they carry a great deal of energy. One day in 2005 the large iceberg that MacAyeal had been studying inexplicably began to slam against the shoreline. It was completely destroyed. A seismometer (vibration-sensing instrument) showed that the iceberg had been struck by a series of low-amplitude waves. MacAyeal believes that storm swells may also destroy ice shelves, such as Larsen B, that are already weakened by surface melting.

Glaciers, Permafrost, Lake Ice . . . Lost

Many of the world's glaciers are also declining. Greenland's massive ice sheet holds one-twentieth of the total volume of Earth's ice, so it provides an important example. Between 2003 and 2007 approximately three times more ice was lost per year from Greenland than was accumulated in snowpack. Temperatures averaged 7 to 11 °F (4–6 °C) above average in the summer of 2007. Many of the island's glaciers feed directly into the ocean. Among these glaciers is Jakobshavn Isbrae, rumored to have calved the iceberg that sank the *Titanic*. It has now gained notoriety as the fastest-moving glacier in the world. Jakobshavn slides forward at a phenomenal rate of 118 feet (36 m) per day, adding 50 billion tons (45 billion tonnes) of ice to Baffin Bay each year. This fast rate of acceleration has also caused the glacier to elongate and grow thinner. Its thickness decreases by about 49 feet (15 m) per year.

Nowhere on Earth are glaciers more magnificent than on Asia's Tibetan Plateau. At least 17,000 glaciers sit on the high slopes of this region, known as "the roof of the world." The meltwater produced from the slopes each spring feeds five of the largest rivers in the world—the Ganges, Indus, Mekong, Yangtze, and Yellow rivers—which in turn provide water for drinking, cooking, bathing, irrigation, industry, and more to billions of people living downstream. Ice cores taken beginning in the 1980s reveal that, like other parts of the cryosphere, the plateau is warming. The average warming is more than 0.5 °F (0.3 °C) per decade since the 1950s.

Baffin Bay holds 50 billion tons (45 billion tonnes) of ice per year deposited by the Jakobshavn glacier.

Temperature increase seems closely associated with a reduction in snowpack, and the outcome is painfully obvious. A review of glaciers across the plateau shows that more than 80 percent are retreating, or losing ice. According to a 2004 report called the Chinese Glacier Inventory, this rate of melting will result in complete melting of all that country's glaciers by the end of the century.

Residents of Alaska have noticed the changes in different ways. Much of the Alaskan landscape is made up of permafrost. Technically, permafrost is soil that remains frozen (at or below 32 °F [0 °C]) for at least two years. In Alaska permafrost may have been in place for more than 120,000 years. Homes and other buildings, pipelines, roads, and railroads are built atop it. The top few inches or even feet may routinely melt in summer, the melted ice allowing plants to grow—but then the water quickly freezes again in winter. (This annual melt-and-thaw cycle also explains why much of the Arctic can support only small plants such as those found on the tundra.) Permafrost soils have responded to the warming of Arctic air temperatures. Since the 1980s the Alaskan permafrost has warmed by 3 to 6 °F (1.7–3.3 °C). Shallow-rooted trees tilt as the hard soil grows soft; families and businesses have been forced to move because of the resulting cracking in the foundations of their buildings. The Inupiaq people on Alaska's Sarichef Island have been forced to relocate the village where their families have lived and hunted for four hundred years. The NOAA reports the reason:

> [R]ising temperatures [are] causing a reduction in sea ice, [and] thawing of permafrost along the coast. The reduced sea ice allows higher storm surges to reach shore and thawing permafrost makes the shoreline more vulnerable to erosion. The town's homes, water system and infrastructure are being undermined.

Permafrost is also thawing on the Tibetan Plateau. Among structures at risk is the Qinghai-Xizang Railroad, only recently built to allow easier travel between Tibet and cities elsewhere in China. The railroad passes over large regions of permafrost, more than half of which is within 3.6 °F (2 °C) of the freezing point. A continuing temperature rise on the plateau will inevitably cause thawing under the railway bed and damage to the line.

Seasonal portions of the cryosphere have been impacted, as well. Lake Superior is the world's largest body of fresh water. The recording of its temperature dates back more than a hundred years, during which the lake's average annual

Earth's
Changing
Climate

A house collapses near Portage Glacier, Alaska, as the permafrost beneath it thaws.

temperature has increased by 6 °F (3.3 °C). Researchers from the Large Lakes Observatory found that three-quarters of this warming has taken place since 1980. During that same time period, winter ice cover on the lake has also declined noticeably. Many of the lakes' natural processes and organisms are adapted for cold. Ever higher temperatures in summer put them at increasing risk.

Five

What Does It Mean to Me?

In 1988 Dr. James Hansen of NASA's Goddard Institute for Space Studies was asked to speak before Congress about climate change. The topic was not a popular one. Many people did not believe that global warming was happening at all, and no one was eager to hear that it could be the result of human actions. A physicist named Mark Bowen described the moment when Hansen met the press after talking to Congress:

> "It's time to stop waffling so much and say that the greenhouse effect is here and is affecting our climate now," [said Hansen.]
>
> This apocalyptic warning, delivered in a monotone by a matter-of-fact, almost bland Midwesterner, on a day when the temperature broke one hundred degrees in downtown Washington, flashed across television screens and made newspaper headlines around the world.

Simply put, human contributions of greenhouse gases are responsible for global warming, and warming leads to climate change. There are six main greenhouse gases (GHGs). Four of these—water vapor, carbon dioxide, methane, and nitrous oxide—may be produced naturally or by human activities. Tropospheric ozone and fluorinated gases are made only by humans. It is important to note that there are two subgroups of ozone. Tropospheric ozone is the type found near the planet's surface. It causes smog. Stratospheric, or upper atmospheric, ozone helps to reflect sunlight. Fluorinated gases include hydrofluorocarbons, perfluorocarbons, and sulfur hexafluoride. These gases are the by-products of industry. Although fluorinated gases occur in low concentrations, they have a proportionately greater effect on global warming.

A Closer Look at Greenhouse Gases

According to the IPCC, 75 percent of human-made CO_2 emissions come from fossil fuel combustion (burning of coal, natural gas, and oil). Most of the remaining emissions result from deforestation (large-scale cutting of trees). Proxy records indicate that just prior to the Industrial Revolution (mid–1700s), CO_2 levels were 280 ppm. The 2008 concentration was 385.57 ppm, an increase of 1.86 ppm over the previous year. In the long record of climate change, it has typically taken at least one thousand years for CO_2 concentration to increase by 30 ppm. Carbon dioxide emissions are now increasing so rapidly that it takes less than twenty years to increase the concentration by 30 ppm.

For decades the United States has held a dubious record as the world's top emitter of CO_2. In 2006 China stepped up to take that title. China is home to more than 1.3 billion people. As its economy continues to become much more industrialized, Chinese citizens want more goods and services. Production and sales of cell phones, televisions, computers, and much more require electricity. Electricity is also used to build products that are shipped for sale in the United States. Between 2002 and 2006 more than 560 new coal-fired electrical plants were built worldwide. Carbon dioxide emissions rose by one billion tons (0.9 billion tonnes) per year as a result. China constructed two-thirds of these plants. Yet the United States, with its much smaller population, has a carbon dioxide

安 慧 桥 ⑸ 1 km
ANHUI Bridge

惠 新 东 桥 ㊾ 2 km
HUIXIN East Bridge

望 和 桥 ❶ 4 km
WANGHE Bridge

出 口
EXIT ↗

北辰路
BEICHEN Rd

China has taken strides toward reducing carbon dioxide emissions by producing fuel efficient cars.

"footprint" much larger than China's. On average, an American emits more than four times as much CO_2 per year than a Chinese citizen. In vehicles, carbon dioxide emissions correlate to fuel efficiency. In 2004 China took steps to reduce its transportation emissions. China's newly designed fuel-efficiency standards have the most impact on heavy cars (such as trucks and sport utility vehicles). Overall reductions in fuel consumption were also required by the standards. By contrast, average fuel economy has changed very little in the United States since the 1980s. Passenger cars and trucks contribute 20 percent of total CO_2 emissions in the United States.

Nitrous oxide comes mainly from fertilizers. Additional sources are the burning of fossil fuels and other materials, some industrial processes, and wastewater treatment. Methane is produced in landfills. Agricultural sources include rice paddies and cattle. It may sound funny to hear that cows belch methane while digesting grass and grains, but a single cow produces up to 242 pounds (110 kilograms) of methane per year. The U.S. Environmental Protection Agency calculates that worldwide, methane emission from cattle totals more than 88 million tons (80 million tonnes)—about 28 percent of all human-related methane.

Worldwide, cattle produce 88 million tons (80 million tonnes) of methane per year.

Tropospheric ozone is made during the chemical reaction between sunlight, nitrogen oxides, and volatile organic compounds (VOCs), a large group of gases produced by natural and industrial processes. Methane is a VOC; so are benzene (in gasoline fumes) and formaldehyde (a preservative that is also used in many industrial fluids, such as paint). Halocarbons, a complex group of human-made gases containing carbon along with chlorine, bromine, or fluorine, were developed as refrigerants and industrial chemicals. In the late 1970s it was discovered that chlorine-containing chemicals, known as CFCs and HCFCs, had broken down large amounts of stratospheric ozone. The result was a large "hole" in the ozone layer over Antarctica. Bromine-containing halogens had the same effect. The production and use of all these chemicals has been phased out under an international agreement called the Montreal Protocol. The ozone hole is now slowly improving.

There are two major concerns related to greenhouse gas emissions. The first has to do with balance. These gases naturally occur at very low concentrations in Earth's atmosphere—so small that they are measured in molecules per million or billion. At such low concentrations, even a small increase can result in a large effect. Carbon and nitrogen move between the atmosphere, water, soil and rocks, and living things in finely tuned cycles. When humans disrupt these cycles, the impacts on climate can be many-layered. For example, deforestation is a major cause of increased concentrations of carbon dioxide because trees use CO_2 during photosynthesis. The felled trees may also increase concentrations if they are burned, as burning releases additional carbon that was held in their tissues. In addition, exposed soil at logging sites is more vulnerable to evaporation, which may alter the local humidity and precipitation patterns.

The second problem is that GHGs can endure in the upper atmosphere for many years. Methane is the shortest-lived molecule; its lifetime is about twelve years. Some of the halogen-containing gases persist for thousands of years. (see Table 1). Each greenhouse gas has a different impact on warming—it produces a certain amount of radiative forcing.

More on Greenhouse Gases

Despite their bad reputation, greenhouse gases are critical to life on Earth. Scientists believe that without them, Earth's surface temperature might be 59°F (33°C) colder. There are many natural sources of greenhouse gases.

- Carbon dioxide: Any organic material that is burned produces CO_2. It also moves through the carbon cycle. It is produced by the respiration of plants and animals, by decomposition, by volcanic eruptions, and by release from oceans.

- Methane: Decomposition in wetlands is a significant source of methane. It is also present in the oceans and can be emitted during wildfires. Termites are another interesting source: like cows, they give it off during their digestion of wood. Permafrost is a large sink for methane. A sink is a location in which a large amount of the gas is held. Scientists believe that thawing permafrost in the Arctic and other cold regions may release large amounts of methane very quickly.

- Nitrous oxide: Nitrous oxide is released from the soils by bacteria. Like the other gases, it also evaporates from the oceans.

These impacts are assigned values, which scientists call global warming potentials. The global warming potential of carbon dioxide is 1. This value provides a basis of comparison for all other GHGs. Potentials vary depending on the period of time being discussed. For example, methane has a hundred-year global warming potential of 21—over a period of a hundred years, it can create twenty-one times more radioactive forcing than carbon dioxide. What it lacks in global warming potential, carbon dioxide makes up for in sheer volume. Worldwide, electrical power plants produce more than 11 billion tons (10 billion tonnes) of CO_2 each year.

What Does the Future Hold?

The IPCC has compiled forty scenarios for global warming based on human carbon dioxide emissions, resource use, and changes in technology, economy, and population, among other markers. Each scenario produces a different outcome for climate change. The most extreme scenarios look at what happens if no action is taken. In this case, global temperatures may increase 4.3 to 11.5 °F (2.4–6.4 °C) by the year 2100,

A chimney at an electrical substation belches smoke containing CO_2 and other gases.

Table 1. Lifetimes and Global Warming Potentials of Representative Greenhouse Gases

Greenhouse Gas	Lifetime in the Atmosphere (years)	Global Warming Potential (100-year)
Carbon dioxide	50–200	1
Methane	~12	21
Nitrous oxide	120	310
Hydrofluorochloride-21 (HFC-23)	264	11,700
Chlorofluorocarbon (CF_4)	50,000	6,500
Sulfur hexafluoride (SF_6)	3,200	23,900

Source: U.S. EPA, 2002.

with a sea level rise of 0.85 to 1.9 feet (0.26–0.59 m). (These values are relative to average temperatures and sea levels from 1980 to 1999.) The highest degree of action emphasizes sustainability. It could limit global warming to a range of 2 to 5.2 °F (1.1–2.9 °C) and sea level rise to between 0.6 and 1.2 feet (0.18–0.38 m). The long lifetimes of greenhouse gases explain why temperature will rise for a while, even under the "sustainability" scenario. In other words, Earth's climate and systems will change, to some degree, no matter how much emissions are reduced today. The reality is that over the next few decades, climate-related challenges will require human ingenuity, cooperation, and patience. Here are some of the possible outcomes.

Albedo

Albus is the Latin word for "white." White surfaces reflect light very well. Dark-colored surfaces (such as the blue ocean) tend to absorb sunlight. Albedo is often given on a scale of 0 to 1, with brighter surfaces receiving values closer to 1. (There are no units.) The albedo of fresh snow may be as high as 0.95. The albedo of clouds can also be high, measuring up to 0.7. Grass and asphalt typically measure very low albedo, and water may measure as low as 0.02 on the albedo scale. For thousands of years the cryosphere has played a role in controlling global temperature by reflecting some of the sunlight that enters Earth's atmosphere. As snow and ice melts, it reveals more low-albedo surfaces, such as open water and soil. Scientists may now know why Earth's cold regions seem to be warming almost four times faster than the global average.

Since the Industrial Revolution began in the mid–1700s, average warming in the Arctic has been 6.3 °F (3.5 °C) compared with the calculated average global warming of 1.3 °F (0.74 °C). Losses of pack ice, ice shelves, and glaciers are not the only sources of albedo: seasonal ice and snow from regions of the cryosphere impact the total amount of sunlight that is reflected. The IPCC states that snow cover has changed in the Northern Hemisphere. Since 1966 early spring snows have declined by about 2 percent per decade.

Sea Level Rise

At the height of the Wisconsinan, sea level was about 410 feet (125 m) below its current level because most of the water was frozen into ice sheets. Because of the lower sea level, shorelines on all the continents were much farther out than they are today. As this ice age ended, the glaciers began to melt. Water gradually refilled the ocean and lake basins. This same process will take place if glaciers melt now. The difference is that coastlines are now highly populated. Scientists warn that the Greenland ice sheet is so large that if it melts completely, global sea level would increase by 21 feet (6.5 m). Antarctica has three major glacier sources: the peninsula, the eastern ice sheet, and the western ice sheet. Together they could add more than 240 feet (73 m) to sea level. The world's remaining constrained glaciers contain enough water to add another 1.6 feet (0.5 m).

Fast-moving glaciers deposit more icebergs into the ocean. This addition of ice from land can affect sea level. Larsen B acted as a dam to only a few glaciers, but ice shelves on the western side of Antarctica hold back many dozens. The Ross and the Ronne are each larger than California. If either collapsed, it would expose glaciers containing enough ice to gradually increase global sea level by more than 16 feet (5 m). In 2000 NASA's Goddard Institute for Space Studies reported that "eleven of the world's 15 largest cities lie along the coast or on estuaries." In total, one-tenth of the human population lives in coastal areas with elevations less than 33 feet (10 m) above sea level. Some of the Maldive Islands, in the Indian Ocean, have already begun to experience shoreline erosion as a result of rising water. With an average height of only 5 feet (1.5 m) above sea level, they face being completely swept under seas that rise from major glacial melting.

Flooding

Sea level rise may bring flooding to coastlines worldwide, both from glacier melting and thermal expansion. Many nations will face a serious challenge. In the Netherlands—a name that means "the lowlands," an appropriate description

Flood barriers were installed along the village of Itteren, in the Netherlands, to protect it from rising waters of the Maas River.

since most of the country sits below sea level—flooding of cities and fields has so far been prevented by pumping, damming, and diverting water. Innovation is now the key to its survival. The government has responded by purchasing land along rivers in order to prevent people from building on the floodplain. Citizens have new options for housing, as well, including homes that sit on stilts and can rise up if water floods beneath them. Flooding also results from additional precipitation, which occurs in some areas that have higher temperatures.

Fresh Water

In many parts of the world, glaciers are a significant source of fresh water that can be used for drinking, household needs, irrigation, hydropower dams, industry, and more. Glaciers also supply water to downstream ecosystems. As they become smaller, these regions will face serious water shortages. For example, the NSIDC reports that glaciers in the state of Washington produce 470 billion gallons (1.8 trillion liters) of summer meltwater. Since 1980 rainfall has declined by 15 percent in eastern African nations. Recent studies by NASA suggest that a feedback is responsible. Evaporation over the land brings rainfall to the ocean. As the rainfall warms the ocean water, the resulting air movement patterns that are created block the circulation of moisture back onto land. Without a source of rain, the land warms further.

Changes in the Seasons

In the Northern Hemisphere snow and ice have declined as temperatures have warmed—but so have the seasons. Lakes and rivers have been freezing later, by approximately six days per century. The ice also breaks up about six days earlier. Thus, on average, Northern Hemisphere winters have been shortened by eighteen days since record keeping began in the mid–1800s. Shorter winters mean longer growing seasons for crops; the consequent increase in the number of warm days can further increase radiative heating. As in Minnesota, this may cause either evaporation or excess precipitation, depending on the landscape. Earlier spring melt and longer, warmer summers can also increase the risk of fires. The 2006 fire season set a record in the United States, with almost 100,000 fires breaking out and 10 million acres (4 million hectares) burned.

Loss of Species

Scientists have identified and named approximately 1.8 million species so far. The true diversity of life on Earth is not fully known, as scientists are still working to explore many challenging habitats. Estimates range from 3.6 to 112 million in total. Every year new wonders reveal themselves. Some are minuscule bacteria or soil organisms; others are long-hidden birds, delicate flowering plants, or mysterious sea creatures. Dr. Terry Root of Stanford University reviewed 143 studies done on more than 1,450 species of plants, birds, mammals, and mollusks. She was particularly interested in how these species responded to global warming. Evidence she turned up indicated that 80 percent of the species had begun to shift their ranges (the area over which the species is found). Some had begun to move north; others were moving up mountains. The species appear to be shifting their ranges as climate change affects their traditional habitats. Many of these species have small but vital "jobs" in the environment. So little is known about many plants and animals that it is impossible to predict the effects of a species' extinction on the ecosystem or on humans. Did it pollinate a valuable food source? Did its cells hold a cure for disease?

As temperatures change, some species have shifted their migratory patterns and habitats.

80

Reducing the Effect

The good news is that there are many ways to reduce the impact of global warming. These solutions come from all areas of society: government, industry, and citizens. Perhaps the most extensive response was the Kyoto Protocol:

> The Kyoto Protocol is an international agreement linked to the United Nations Framework Convention on Climate Change. The major feature of the Kyoto Protocol is that it sets binding targets for 37 industrialized countries and the European community for reducing greenhouse gas (GHG) emissions. These amount to an average of five per cent against 1990 levels over the five-year period 2008–2012.

> The major distinction between the Protocol and the Convention is that while the Convention **encouraged** industrialised countries to stabilize GHG emissions, the Protocol **commits** them to do so.

The United States did not sign the Kyoto Protocol but may choose to reduce greenhouse gases in different ways in the future.

A government can exercise several options to reduce greenhouse gas emissions. The most basic is a tax, whereby the government adds a percentage to the cost of items that produce greenhouse gases. Industries, businesses, and consumers pay the tax, and the government uses the money to clean up the problem. The government also expects the higher price to discourage use of the item. Few people like taxes, however, so this approach does not get much support. Regulations are essentially laws that could stop greenhouse gas emissions before they start. Some are already in place—fuel-efficiency standards are an example. Regulations can be effective to some extent, but in most nations (especially those that are proud of having a lot of independence in business, such as the United States), they can be hard to pass.

81

Governments can also invest. For example, a city government might fund projects that install "green" roofs on buildings. (These roofs are made of plant material instead of blacktop. They cut down on heat absorption and thus reduce the need for air conditioning.) Most investments come from business, but governments can assist in this process. Incentives are an additional option. They provide a reward to consumers and businesses that reduce emissions. Tax incentives were offered to encourage sales of hybrid cars in the United States. In 2008 Israel offered a similar deal to citizens who agreed to purchase electric cars.

Cap-and-trade systems are generally considered the best way to reduce greenhouse gas emissions. A cap (limit) is set on the total number of emissions for each gas. Companies are given permits for emissions, which they can trade. This system allows some companies to make a profit for reducing emissions; companies that do not reduce can pay to obtain additional permits. The total number of permits declines each year, until the emissions goal is reached. A carbon dioxide cap-and-trade program was started by the European Union in 2005. In May 2008 signatory nations of the Kyoto Protocol traded 1.1 million tons (1 million tonnes) of carbon dioxide. In that same year, ten U.S. states were members of the Regional Greenhouse Gas Initiative (RGGI). RGGI has a mandatory cap-and-trade system that requires 10 percent reductions of CO_2 by 2018.

Waking Up

Climate change has not resulted from the actions of one person or even one nation. Nevertheless, the actions of individuals can help reduce global warming. Every time people choose to pull the plug on an appliance or piece of electronic equipment that is not in use, they make an impact. Lowering fuel consumption by walking, biking, carpooling, taking public transportation, or choosing an alternative vehicle will help the tally sheet on CO_2 go down a notch. Choices at the store also send a strong message. Manufacturers and stores pay attention when people select sustainable products; two examples that

Everyone can contribute to reducing carbon dioxide emissions. One way is by riding bikes.

make a big impact are items with minimal plastic and paper packaging and organic foods that do not use chemical fertilizers. The right to vote is equally important. By playing an active role in choosing lawmakers, people exercise control over funding and decisions that affect their society, health, and environment.

At times we all feel the weight of this responsibility. No one is expected to change the world alone. If you have just begun to learn about climate change, consider setting a few goals with your family and friends. Here are some simple suggestions:

- Buy compact fluorescent or LED lightbulbs for home use; they emit less carbon dioxide than standard incandescent bulbs.

- Turn off lights in empty rooms to reduce electricity consumption. Heating and air conditioning are other electricity hogs, so try adjusting the thermostat by two degrees—lower in winter and higher in summer months.

- Choose produce and meats that are raised close to home rather than those imported over long distances.

- Ride a bike or walk when traveling short distances. These activities provide exercise while reducing vehicle emissions.

Those already inspired to live a bit more sustainably might join a school organization (or start one) to help inform others about climate change prevention. Preparing for college? Add "green" to your checklist of priorities when looking at schools. Every year more colleges and universities, in the United States and worldwide, adopt programs to reduce their impact on climate change and related environmental risks. There are also a variety of courses and degree programs that prepare students to live and work in a changing world.

At least five hundred years ago, leaders of the Iroquois Confederacy, a group of American-Indian nations in the northeastern United States, prepared a constitution that would unite their nations into a single, peaceful democratic society. Written into this constitution was a timeless reminder.

> Look and listen for the welfare of the whole people and have always in view not only the present but also the coming generations, even those whose faces are yet beneath the surface of the ground—the unborn of the future Nation.

Working as a whole people, we can reduce the impact of global climate change and make Earth a healthy home for generations to come.

Notes

Chapter One

p. 9, "The morning temperature of 49 degrees Fahrenheit...": "Preliminary Local Climatological Data—Chanhassen, MN." Minnesota Climatology Working Group, January 2, 2009, http://climate.umn.edu/doc/prelim_lcd_mpx.htm (accessed October 28, 2009).

p. 9, "On average, air temperatures in the state have increased by 1 to 2 °F...": Zandlo (2008).

p. 9, "Global temperature records have been collected since the 1850s...": IPCC 2007, *Climate Change 2007: The Physical Science Basis. Contribution of Working Group I to the Fourth Assessment Report of the Intergovernmental Panel on Climate Change*, eds. S. Solomon, D. Qin, M. Manning, Z. Chen, M. Marquis, K. B. Averyt, M. Tignor, and H. L. Miller (New York: Cambridge University Press, 2007), ch. 4.

p. 11, "... average global temperature increased by 1.3 °F...": IPCC (2007), ch. 3.

p. 11, "... the century's hottest years have all taken place since 1990.": "2007 Was Tied as Earth's Second-Warmest Year," National Aeronautics and Space Administration,

January 16, 2008, www.nasa.gov/centers/goddard/ news/topstory/2008/earth_temp.html (accessed July 21, 2008).

p. 11, "… temperatures are 14 °F (7.8 °C) higher at the southern end of Minnesota …": John Tester, *Minnesota's Natural Heritage* (Minneapolis: University of Minnesota Press, 1995), p. 30.

p. 12, "According to the Minnesota Pollution Control Agency,…": "Global Warming and Climate Change in Minnesota." Minnesota Pollution Control Agency, November 2003, http://proteus.pca.state.mn.us/oea/reduce/climatechange. cfm (accessed September 1, 2008).

p. 13, "Germany also has a continental climate. Temperatures there…": Marc Zebisch et al., "Climate Change in Germany: Vulnerability and Adaptation Strategies of Climate-Sensitive Sectors," German Federal Environmental Agency, n/d., www.umweltdaten.de/ publikationen/fpdf-k/k2974.pdf (accessed September 4, 2008).

p. 13, "A study conducted by Tufts University in Medford, Massachusetts, in 2007 indicates that . . .": Elizabeth A. Stanton and Fred Ackerman, "Florida and Climate Change: The Costs of Inaction," Tufts University, November 2007,www.ase.tufts.edu/gdae/Pubs/rp/Florida_ lrExecSummary.pdf (accessed August 31, 2008).

p. 14, "… the overall number of storms in the Atlantic could decline by 2060,…": Willie Drye, "Global Warming to Decrease Hurricanes, Study Says," *National Geographic News*, May 19, 2008, http://news.nationalgeographic. com/news/pf/13243739.html (accessed July 27, 2008).

p. 14, "… hurricanes will grow stronger in response to warmer ocean temperatures.": Willie Drye, "Strong Hurricanes Getting Stronger; Warming Is Blamed,"

National Geographic News, September 4, 2008, http://news.nationalgeographic.com/news/2008/09/080904-warming-hurricanes.html (accessed September 4, 2008).

p. 14, "... ocean water has warmed by approximately 0.5 °F (0.28 °C).": Drye, "Strong Hurricanes Getting Stronger" (accessed September 4, 2008).

p. 15, "The Intergovernmental Panel on Climate Change (IPCC) reports on the effects of ocean warming...": IPCC (2007), ch. 5.

p. 16, "Wilma made the record books as the most intense Atlantic storm...": "Climate of 2005—Atlantic Hurricane Season," NOAA Satellite and Information Service, August 21, 2006, www.ncdc.noaa.gov/oa/climate/research/2005/hurricanes05.html (accessed August 29, 2007).

p. 17, "For the 2008 hurricane season, meteorologists predicted...": Philip J. Klotzbach and William M. Gray, "Extended Range Forecast of Atlantic Seasonal Hurricane Activity and U.S. Landfall Strike Probability for 2008," Colorado State University, December 7, 2007, http://hurricane.atmos.colostate.edu/Forecasts/2007/dec2007/dec2007.pdf (accessed August 29, 2008).

p. 17, "On a single day, September 2, four storms...": "2008 Hurricane Season Kicks into High Gear," NASA Earth Observatory News, September 4, 2008, http://earthobservatory.nasa.gov/Newsroom/NasaNews/2008/2008090427398.html (accessed September 5, 2008).

p. 18, "In its 2007 report the IPCC stated...": IPCC (2007).

p. 19, "The U.S. Environmental Protection Agency (EPA) further explains how global warming...": "Climate Change—Health and Environmental Effects." U.S. Environmental

Protection Agency, December 20, 2007, www.epa.gov/climatechange/effects/index.html (accessed August 2, 2008).

p. 20, "In the 1950s Revelle had begun studying the role of carbon dioxide...": Mark Bowen, *Thin Ice: Unlocking the Secrets of Climate in the World's Highest Mountains* (New York: Henry Holt, 2005), p. 109.

p. 21, "In May 1958 Keeling obtained CO_2 readings...": "The Early Keeling Curve," Scripps Institute of Oceanography, 2009, http://scrippsco2.ucsd.edu/program_history/early_keeling_curve.html (accessed September 27, 2009).

p. 22, "Monitoring of CO_2 levels has continued...": R. F. Keeling et al., "Atmospheric CO_2 concentrations (ppm) derived from in situ air measurements at Mauna Loa Observatory, Hawaii," Scripps Institute of Oceanography, 2009, http://scrippsco2.ucsd.edu/data/in_situ_co2/monthly_mlo/csv? (accessed September 27, 2009).

p. 22, "In 2007 he and the IPCC...": "The Nobel Peace Prize 2007," Nobel Foundation, n/d., http://nobelprize.org/nobel_prizes/peace/laureates/2007/ (accessed September 1, 2009).

p. 23, "In *An Inconvenient Truth*, he writes...": Al Gore, *An Inconvenient Truth* (Emmaus, PA: Rodale Press, 2006), p. 161.

Chapter Two
p. 25, "By 2.3 billion years ago, the levels of carbon dioxide had fallen so low...": William K. Stevens, *The Change in the Weather: People, Weather, and the Science of Climate* (New York: Delta, 1999), pp. 9–10.

p. 25, "... glaciers spread from both poles to near the equator. Global average temperatures...": Bowen (2005), p. 93.

p. 25, "Two theories explain how the planet warmed…": "'Snowball Earth' Was More a Slushball," *Discovery News*, December 5, 2007, http://dsc.discovery.com/news/2007/12/05/snowball-earth-climate.html. (accessed August 23, 2008).

p. 25, "In 2009 the global average temperature…": "State of the Climate," NOAA Satellite and Information Service, September 2009, www.ncdc.noaa.gove/sotc/index.php (accessed November 2, 2009).

p. 25, "During parts of the Cretaceous, average global temperatures.": Stevens, p. 14.

p. 28, "The eruption of Indonesia's Mount Tambora in 1815…": Michael Sullivan, "Mount Tambora Explosion Hardly Known," National Public Radio, October 27, 2008, www.npr.org/templates/story/story.php?storyId = 15691309 (accessed July 23, 2008).

p. 29, "Fossil records suggest that in the Cretaceous, carbon dioxide…": "Sea Die-Out Blamed on Volcanoes," BBC News, July 16, 2008, http://news.bbc.co.uk/2/hi/science/nature/7510541.stm (accessed July 29, 2008).

p. 30, "Dust created by the rapid rise of the Tibetan Plateau…": An Zhisheng et al., "Evolution of Asian Monsoons and Phased Uplift of the Himalaya-Tibetan Plateau since Late Miocine Times," *Nature*, May 3, 2001, pp. 62–66.

p. 30, "A change in ocean currents could also have sped up . . .": N. W. Driscoll and G. H. Haug, "A Short Circuit in Thermohaline Circulation: A Cause for Northern Hemisphere Glaciation?" *Science*, October 16, 1998, pp. 436–438.

p. 30, "… ice extended from the North Pole as far south as 45 degrees north latitude": Eric B. Taylor, "Zoogeography:

The Physical Setting—Glaciation," University of British Columbia, May 2007, www.zoology.ubc.ca/~etaylor/413www/glaciation.html (accessed September 7, 2008).

p. 30, "Ice blanketed as much as 32 percent...": "All about Glaciers," National Snow and Ice Data Center, n/d., www.nsidc.org/glaciers/ (accessed July 29, 2008).

p. 30, "Where Chicago now sits, a sheet of ice 1 mile (1.6 km) thick...": "Landforms Tell the Story," Illinois Department of Natural Resources, 2008, http://dnr.state.il.us/Lands/Landmgt/PARKS/I&M/CORRIDOR/geo/geo.htm (accessed August 2, 2008).

p. 30, "Sea level was at least 394 feet (120 meters) lower...": Vivien Gornitz, "Sea Level Rise, after the Ice Melted and Today," NASA Goddard Institute for Space Studies, January 2007, www.giss.nasa.gov/research/briefs/gornitz_09/ (accessed August 12, 2008).

p. 32, "Earth has about a 3-degree range in its tilt...": Bowen, pp. 280–282.

p. 33, "Researchers were able to match the dates of coral fossils to glacial events.": Wallace S. Broecker et al., "Milankovitch Hypothesis Supported by Precise Dating of Coral Reefs and Deep-Sea Sediments," *Science*, January 19, 1968, pp. 297–300, www.sciencemag.org/cgi/content/abstract/159/3812/297 (accessed August 16, 2008).

p. 33, "Ice cores taken from Vostok Station, near the South Pole...": Brian Fagan, *The Long Summer: How Climate Changed Civilization* (New York: Basic Books, 2004), pp. 23–24.

Chapter Three
p. 35, "As the Wisconsinan ice sheets began to withdraw...": Stevens, p. 26.

p. 35, "The Vostok cores show that carbon dioxide levels dip as low…": Fagan (2004), p. 23.

p. 35, "…a temperature spike of 15 °F (8.3 °C) that took place in just ten years.": Lorraine A. Remer, "Explaining Rapid Climate Change: Tales from the Ice," NASA Earth Observatory, n/d., http://earthobservatory.nasa.gov/Study/Paleoclimatology_Evidence/paleoclimatology_evidence_2.html (accessed September 1, 2008).

p. 35, "Antarctic ice cores also confirm that greenhouse gases…": Renato Spahni et al., "Atmospheric Methane and Nitrous Oxide of the Late Pleistocene from Antarctic Ice Cores," *Science*, November 25, 2005, pp. 1317–1321.

p. 37, "As the region's population increased, competition…": Fagan (2004), pp. xiv–xv.

p. 37, "By 3200 BCE, Uruk had an early form of government,…": "Uruk—The First City," Metropolitan Museum of Art, 2008, www.metmuseum.org/toah/hd/uruk/hd_uruk.htm (accessed August 23, 2008).

p. 37, "Beginning in 900 CE and continuing for a period of about four hundred years,…": Fagan (2004), p. 211.

p. 37, "The great Mayan civilization, located on Mexico's…": Stefan Lovgren, "Climate Change Killed Off Maya Civilization, Study Says," *National Geographic News*, March 13, 2003, http://news.nationalgeographic.com/news/2003/03/0313_030313_mayadrought.html (accessed July 19, 2008).

p. 37, "The Little Ice Age began around 1300 and lasted until 1850.": Brian Fagan, *The Little Ice Age: How Climate Made History, 1300–1850* (New York: Basic Books, 2000), ch. 3.

p. 39, "A significant outcome of the Little Ice Age was...": Barbara Freese, *Coal: A Human History* (New York: Penguin Books, 2003), ch. 2, 3, and 8.

p. 40, "Eighteenth-century British engineers began to design...": Freese, ch. 3.

p. 40, "In 2007 scientists from the IPCC...": IPCC (2007), ch. 9.

p. 41, "The eruption of Mount Agung on Bali...": James E. Hansen et al., "Mount Agung Eruption Provides a Test of a Global Climatic Perturbation," *Science*, March 10, 1978, pp. 1065–1068, http://pubs.giss.nasa.gov/docs/1978/1978_Hansen_etal.pdf (accessed July 10, 2008).

p. 42, "In 2004 NASA scientists calculated that global temperature fluctuates...": "Solar Variability: Striking a Balance with Climate Change," *NASA*, May 7, 2008, www.nasa.gov/topics.solarsystem/features/solar-variability.html (accessed October 20, 2009).

Chapter Four

p. 43, "Born in the early 1450s, Cabot became a spice merchant...": "John Cabot," Newfoundland and Labrador Heritage, 2000, www.heritage.nf.ca/exploration/cabot.html (accessed September 2, 2008).

p. 43, "In 1496 Cabot met a group of merchants who offered...": Laurence Bergreen, "Excerpt: *Over the Edge of the World*," National Public Radio, July 13, 2005, www.npr.org/templates/story/story.php?storyId = 4723515 (accessed September 3, 2008).

p. 44, "In 1845 Franklin set forth, with more than 128 men...": PBS (2006).

p. 45, "In 1497, on his second attempt, Cabot...": Newfoundland and Labrador Heritage (2000).

p. 45, "Almost 350 years after Cabot's death, the British Royal Navy…": *NOVA*, "Arctic Passage," PBS, 2006, www.pbs.org/wgbh/nova/arctic/ (accessed September 2, 2008).

p. 47, "Half a century later, in 1903, a thirty-year-old sailor named Roald Amundsen…": PBS (2006).

p. 48, "Pack ice forms when seawater reaches its freezing point…": "Sea Ice," National Aeronautics and Space Administration, February 20, 2008, http://nasascience.nasa.gov/earth-science/oceanography/physical-ocean/sea-ice (accessed August 17, 2008).

p. 49, "Currently, glaciers cover 10 percent of all land surface and hold…": "Glacier Story: Quick Facts," National Snow and Ice Data Center, n/d., http://nsidc.org/glaciers/quickfacts.html (accessed August 30, 2008).

p. 49, "Sections of the ice sheet on Greenland, a massive island…": Gary Braasch, *Earth under Fire: How Global Warming Is Changing the World* (Berkeley: University of California Press, 2007), p. 18.

p. 49, "…(EPICA) drilled a 2-mile (3.2-km) ice core…": Laetitia Loulergue et al., "Orbital and Millennial-Scale Features of Atmospheric CH_4 over the Past 800,000 Years," *Nature*, May 15, 2008, pp. 383–386.

p. 49, "The Arctic core showed a five-year period in the 1840s…": PBS (2006).

p. 51, "The first measurements, taken by submarine in 1958, showed that perennial ice…": Braasch, p. 21.

p. 51, "They obtained an average of 2.7 million square miles…": "Arctic Sea Ice Shatters All Previous Record Lows," National Snow and Ice Data Center, October 1, 2007, http://nsidc.org/news/press/2007_seaiceminimum/20071001_pressrelease.html (accessed August 3, 2008).

p. 51, "This average is half the Arctic Ocean's total area…": "Arctic Ocean," CIA World Factbook, August 7, 2008, www.cia.gov/library/publications/the-world-factbook/geos/xq.html (accessed August 13, 2008).

p. 51, "It turns out that summer ice in the Arctic Ocean has declined…": National Snow and Ice Data Center (accessed October 1, 2007).

p. 51, "By September 2007 ice extent was down to 1.65 million square miles…": National Snow and Ice Data Center (accessed October 1, 2007).

p. 53, "The Soviet Union (USSR) surprised the world in 1957…": William J. Jordan, "Soviet Fires Earth Satellite into Space; It Is Circling the Globe at 18,000 MPH; Sphere Tracked in Four Crossings over U.S.," *New York Times*, October 5, 1957, www.nytimes.com/partners/aol/special/sputnik/sput-01.html (accessed July 19, 2008).

p. 53, "Though its primary goal was to show that the USSR was ahead…": Brian Dunbar, "Sputnik 1," National Aeronautics and Space Administration, March 23, 2008, www.nasa.gov/multimedia/imagegallery/image_feature_924.html (accessed July 19, 2008).

p. 53, "More than 4,500 satellites have been put into space.": "The Space Age at 50," *Catalyst*, Fall 2000, pp. 5–7.

p. 54, "On August 29, 2007, satellite images revealed very little ice.": "Natural Hazards: Northwest Passage Open," NASA Earth Observatory, August 29, 2007, http://earthobservatory.nasa.gov/NaturalHazards/natural_hazards_v2.php3?img_id = 14479 (accessed September 2, 2008).

p. 54, "Late the next summer, the Northwest Passage opened once again.": "Arctic Shortcuts Open Up; Decline Pace Steady," National Snow and Ice Data Center, August 25,

2008, http://nsidc.org/arcticseaicenews/2008/082508. html (accessed September 4, 2008).

p. 54, "The National Oceanic and Atmospheric Administration's National Ice Center reported the event, noting…": "The Northern Sea Route (Northeast Passage) Appears 'Open,'" National Ice Center, September 5, 2008, www.natice.noaa.gov/press_release/ (accessed September 6, 2008).

p. 54, "… a gigantic "island" of ice in the middle of the Arctic Ocean…": Tom Wright, "Arctic Warming: More Evidence of Melting, Scientists Say," *Wall Street Journal*, September 2, 2008, http://blogs.wsj.com/envi ronmentalcapital/2008/09/02/ (accessed September 4, 2008).

p. 55, "Changes in the large…": "About IPY," International Polar Year, 2007, www.ipy.org/index.php?/ipy/about/ (accessed July 1, 2008).

p. 55, "*Envisat*, orbiting the planet at an altitude of about 500 miles…": "Envisat," European Space Agency Earthnet, 2008, http://envisat.esa.int/category/index. cfm?fcategoryid=87 (accessed August 1, 2008).

p. 56, "More than 150 EOSs currently orbit the planet.": Andrew J. Tatem et al., "Fifty Years of Earth-Observation Satellites," *American Scientist*, September–October 2008, pp. 390–398.

p. 57, "Ice began to calve from the front of Larsen B in the 1990s…": Braasch, pp. 9–11.

p. 57, "… the 12,000-year-old shelf…": Lorraine A. Remer, "Breakup of the Larsen Ice Shelf, Antarctica," NASA Earth Observatory, n/d., http://earthobservatory.nasa. gov/Newsroom/NewImages/images.php3?img_id=8257 (accessed September 4, 2008).

Earth's
Changing
Climate

p. 57, "The Hektoria Glacier had already been accelerating by 0.04 inch...": Lorraine A. Remer, "Glacier Speeds Up after Ice Shelf Collapses," NASA Earth Observatory, n/d., http://earthobservatory.nasa.gov/Newsroom/NewImages/images.php3?img_id=16675 (accessed September 2, 2008).

p. 61, "Antarctica's threshold is 23 °F (–5 °C).": "Larsen Ice Shelf 2002," Portland State University, n/d., http://web.pdx.edu/~ chulbe/science/Larsen/larsen2002.html (accessed August 29, 2008).

p. 61, "On the Antarctic Peninsula, however, temperatures have increased...": Remer, "Breakup of the Larsen Ice Shelf, Antarctica."

p. 61, "Dr. Ted Scambos and his team from the NSIDC...": "Fragment of Its Former Shelf," NASA Earth Observatory, May 28, 2008, http://earthobservatory.nasa.gov/Study/LarsenIceShelf (accessed July 30, 2008).

p. 61, "... unusually strong westerly winds over the Antarctic Peninsula.": "Antarctic Shelf Ice Collapse Tied to Global Warming," Environment News Service, October 16, 2006, http://www.ens-newswire.com/ens/oct2006/2006-10-16-03.asp (accessed July 18, 2008).

p. 61, "... MacAyeal suggests a very different proximate cause of ice shelf collapse.": Laura Naranjo, "After the Larsen B," *Sensing Our Planet: NASA Earth Science Research Features*, 2007, pp. 32–37, http://nasadaacs.eos.nasa.gov/articles/2007/2007_larsen.html (accessed August 12, 2008).

p. 63, "Greenland's massive ice sheet holds one-twentieth of...": Alexandra Witze, "Losing Greenland," *Nature*, April 17, 2008, pp. 798–801.

p. 63, "Jakobshavn slides forward at a phenomenal rate of 118 feet...": "Studying the World's Fastest Flowing Glacier," *Geophysical Institute Quarterly*, 2008, www.gi.alaska. edu/Quarterly/2008/V21N1/2008V21N1.pdf (accessed September 1, 2008).

p. 63, "At least 17,000 glaciers sit on the high slopes...": Evelyne Yohe and Laurie J. Schmidt, "Riding the Permafrost Express," *NASA: Supporting Earth System Science 2005*, 2005, pp. 17–38, http://nasadaacs.eos.nasa.gov/pdf/ annual_2005.pdf (accessed July 16, 2008).

p. 63, "Ice cores taken beginning in the 1980s reveal that...": Jane Qui, "The Third Pole," *Nature*, July 24, 2008, pp. 393–396.

p. 64, "According to a 2004 report called the Chinese Glacier Inventory...": Bowen, p. 391.

p. 65, "In Alaska permafrost may have been in place for more than 120,000 years.": Elizabeth Kolbert, *Field Notes from a Catastrophe: Man, Nature, and Climate Change* (New York: Bloomsbury, 2006), p. 17.

p. 65, "Since the 1980s the Alaskan permafrost has warmed by 3 to 6 °F...": Kolbert, p. 20.

p. 65, "The Inupiaq people on Alaska's Sarichef Island...": "Arctic Change: Human—Shishmaref," National Oceanic and Atmospheric Administration, December 2006, www.arctic.noaa.gov/detect/human-shishmaref. shtml (accessed September 6, 2008).

p. 65, "Among structures at risk is the Qinghai-Xizang Railroad...": Yohe and Schmidt (2005).

p. 65, "... the lake's average annual temperature has increased by 6 °F...": Tim Gihring, "Who Pulled the Plug on Lake Superior?" *Minnesota Monthly*, October 2007, pp. 90–97.

Chapter Five

p. 68, "A physicist named Mark Bowen described the moment...": Bowen, p. 158.

p. 69, "According to the IPCC, 75 percent of human-made CO_2...": IPCC (2007), ch. 7.

p. 69, "... Industrial Revolution (mid-1700s), CO_2 levels were 280 ppm.": "Annual Greenhouse Gas Index (AGGI) Indicates Sharp Rise in Carbon Dioxide and Methane in 2007," NOAA Earth System Research Laboratory, April 23, 2008, www.esrl.nasa.gov/news/2008/aggi.html (accessed July 28, 2008).

p. 69, "... it takes less than twenty years to increase the concentration by 30 ppm.": IPCC (2007), ch. 7.

p. 69, "For decades the United States has held a dubious record...": Richard Harris, "Greenhouse Gas Emissions Rise in China," National Public Radio, July 3, 2008, www.npr.org/templates/story/story.php?storyid = 88251868 (accessed July 3, 2008).

p. 69, "China is home to more than 1.3 billion people.": China Population Information and Research Center, September 10, 2008, www.cpirc.org.cn/en/eindex.htm (accessed September 10, 2008).

p. 69, "Between 2002 and 2006 more than 560 new coal-fired electrical plants...": Mark Clayton, "Global Boom in Coal Power—and Emissions," *Christian Science Monitor*, March 22, 2007, www.csmonitor.com/2007/0322/p01s04-wogi.htm (accessed September 10, 2008).

p. 70, "On average, an American emits more than...": "Energy-Related Carbon Dioxide Emissions," Energy Information Administration, International Energy Outlook 2009, May 29, 2009, www.eia.doe.gov/oiaf/ieo/emissions.html (accessed October 31, 2009).

p. 70, "China's newly designed fuel-efficiency standards...": Amanda Sauer and Fred Wellington, "Taking the High (Fuel Economy) Road," World Resources Institute, November 2004, http://pdf.wri.org/china_the_high_road.pdf (accessed August 18, 2008).

p. 70, "Passenger cars and trucks contribute 20 percent...": "Light-Duty Automotive Technology and Fuel Economy Trends: 1975 through 2007," U.S. Environmental Protection Agency, September 2007, www.epa.gov/OMS/cert/mpg/fetrends/420507001.htm (accessed October 31, 2009.

p. 71, "... a single cow produces up to 242 pounds (110 kilograms) of methane per year.": "Ruminant Livestock—Frequent Questions," U.S. Environmental Protection Agency, March 21, 2007, www.epa.gov/rlep/faq.html (accessed August 19, 2008).

p. 73, "... Earth's surface temperature might be 59 °F (33 °C) colder.": U.S. Environmental Protection Agency (April 2002).

p. 74, "... GHGs can endure in the upper atmosphere for many years.": *Inventory of U.S. Greenhouse Gas Emissions and Sinks: 1990–2000*, U.S. Environmental Protection Agency, Office of Atmospheric Programs, April 2002, www.epa.gov/globalwarming/publications/emissions (accessed August 27, 2008).

p. 74, "Worldwide, electrical power plants produce more than 11 billion tons...": "Carbon Dioxide Emissions from Power Plants Rated Worldwide," *ScienceDaily*, November 15, 2007, www.sciencedaily.com/releases/2007/11/071114163448.htm (accessed September 10, 2008).

p. 74, "The IPCC has compiled forty scenarios for global warming...": IPCC (2007), ch. 10.

p. 76, "The albedo of fresh snow may be as high as 0.95.": David E. Alexander and Rhodes Whitmore Fairbridge, *Encyclopedia of Environmental Science* (New York: Springer, 1999), pp. 15–16.

p. 76, "... seem to be warming almost four times faster ...": Quirin Schiermeier, "The Long Summer Begins," *Nature,* July 17, 2007, pp. 266–269.

p. 76, "The IPCC states that snow cover has changed...": IPCC (2007), ch. 4.

p. 77, "At the height of the Wisconsinan, sea level was...": "Sea Level and Climate," U.S. Geological Survey, January 2000, http://pubs.usgs.gov/fs/fs2-00/ (accessed July 31, 2008).

p. 77, "The Ross and the Ronne are each larger than California. If either collapsed,...": Naranjo (2007).

p. 77, "... "eleven of the world's 15 largest cities lie along the coast or on estuaries."": Vivien Gornitz, "Coastal Populations, Topography, and Sea Level Rise," Goddard Institute for Space Studies, March 2000, www.giss.nasa.gov/research/briefs/gornitz_04/ (accessed September 1, 2008).

p. 77, "In total, one-tenth of the human population lives in coastal areas...": Nell Greenfieldboyce, "Study: 634 Million People at Risk from Rising Seas," *National Public Radio,* March 28, 2007, http://www.npr.org/templates/story/story.php?storyId=9162438 (accessed September 5, 2008).

p. 77, "Some of the Maldive Islands, in the Indian Ocean...": Simon Gardner, "Leader of Imperiled Maldives Issues Stark Warning on Sea Level Rise," *International Herald Tribune,* February 4, 2007. www.iht.com/articles/2007/02/04/news/maldives.php (accessed August 18, 2008).

p. 77, "In the Netherlands—a name that means "the lowlands,"…": Peter Edidin, "Floating Houses Built to Survive Netherlands Floods," *San Francisco Chronicle*, November 9, 2005, www.sfgate.com/cgi-bin/article.cgi?f=/c/a/2005/11/09/HOG9RFI0IJ1.DTL (accessed September 10, 2008).

p. 78, "… glaciers in the state of Washington produce 470 billion gallons…": National Snow and Ice Data Center, n/d.

p. 78, "Since 1980 rainfall has declined by 15 percent…": Lorraine A. Remer, "NASA Data Show Some African Drought Linked to Warmer Indian Ocean," NASA Earth Observatory News, August 5, 2008, http://earthobservatory.nasa.gov/Newsroom/NasaNews/2008/2008080527314.html (accessed September 10, 2008).

p. 79, "Lakes and rivers have been freezing later, by approximately…": IPCC (2007), ch. 4.

p. 79, "The 2006 fire season set a record in the United States…": "Climate of 2006—Wildfire Season Summary," NOAA Satellite and Information Service, January 11, 2007, www.ncdc.noaa.gov/oa/climate/research/2006/fire06.html (accessed July 27, 2008).

p. 79, "Scientists have identified and named approximately 1.9 million…": E. O. Wilson, *The Creation: An Appeal to Save Life on Earth* (New York: Norton, 2006), p. 118.

p. 79, "Dr. Terry Root of Stanford University reviewed 143 studies…": Terry Root et al., "Fingerprints of Global Warming on Wild Animals and Plants," *Nature*, January 2, 2003, pp. 57–60.

p. 81, "Perhaps the most extensive response was the Kyoto Protocol…": "Kyoto Protocol," United Nations Framework Convention on Climate Change, n/d.,

http://unfccc.int/kyoto_protocol/items/2830.php (accessed August 18, 2008).

p. 82, "In 2008 Israel offered a similar deal to citizens who…": Barbara Kiviat, "Israel Looks to Electric Cars," *Time*, January 20, 2008, www.time.com/time/printout/0,8816,1705518,00.html (accessed July 19, 2008).

p. 82, "… signatory nations of the Kyoto Protocol traded 1.1 million tons…": Ovais Subhani, "Kyoto Carbon Trade Hits 1 Million Tonnes a Day," *Reuters*, May 15, 2008, http://uk.reuters.com/article/environmentNews/idUKSP23212420080515 (accessed May 17, 2008).

p. 82, "… the Regional Greenhouse Gas Initiative…": "About RGGI," Regional Greenhouse Gas Initiative, n/d., http://www.rggi.org/ (accessed August 6, 2008).

p. 84, "Look and listen for the welfare…": "The Constitution of the Iroquois Confederacy," Modern History Sourcebook, August 1997, www.fordham.edu/halsall/mod/iroquois.html (accessed October 31, 2009).

Further Information

Books

Cherry, Lynne, and Gary Braasch. *How We Know What We Know about Our Changing Climate: Scientists and Kids Explore Global Warming.* Nevada City, CA: Dawn, 2008.

David, Laurie, and Cambria Gordon. *The Down-to-Earth Guide to Global Warming.* New York: Orchard Books, 2007.

Morris, Neil. *Global Warming.* Milwaukee: World Almanac Library, 2007.

Silverstein, Alvin, Virginia Silverstein, and Laura Silverstein Nunn. *Weather and Climate.* Minneapolis: Twenty-first Century Books, 2008.

DVDs

Global Climate Change. Wynnewood, PA: Schlessinger Media, 2008.

Global Warming: The Signs and the Science. Alexandria, VA: PBS Home Video, 2005.

Earth's Changing Climate

Websites

Climate Change Kids' Site

www.epa.gov/climatechange/kids/index.html

This site, administered by the U.S. Environmental Protection Agency (EPA), takes an age-appropriate approach to the main climate-change topics: weather versus climate, the greenhouse effect, past climates, and humans' impact. Also included are animations of the water and carbon cycles, plus a few links and games.

The Cryosphere at a Glance

http://nsidc.org/cryosphere/glance/

The National Snow and Ice Data Center, based at the University of Colorado at Boulder, offers daily computer images of Earth's permafrost and ice-covered regions.

Global Warming Facts & Our Future

www.koshlandscience.org/exhibitgcc/index.jsp

The Koshland Science Museum website, an arm of the federal government's National Academy of Sciences, provides an officially endorsed introduction to global warming.

Personal Carbon Emissions Calculator

www.epa.gov/climatechange/emissions/ind_calculator.html

At this page of the EPA's site, visitors can determine the volume of greenhouse gases emitted by their household and then find out how they can lower those emissions and save money in doing so.

WeCanSolveIt.org

www.wecansolveit.org/content/homepage/

The home page of the We Campaign, a branch of the Alliance for Climate Protection, an advocacy group whose aim is to convince the public of the need to address climate change by political means. The group's site provides information and support for those who want to learn how to take action in their community.

Bibliography

Alexander, David E., and Rhodes Whitmore Fairbridge. *Encyclopedia of Environmental Science*. New York: Springer, 1999.

Bowen, Mark. *Thin Ice: Unlocking the Secrets of Climate in the World's Highest Mountains*. New York: Henry Holt, 2005.

Braasch, Gary. *Earth under Fire: How Global Warming Is Changing the World*. Berkeley: University of California Press, 2007.

Fagan, Brian. *The Little Ice Age: How Climate Made History, 1300–1850*. New York: Basic Books, 2000.

———. *The Long Summer: How Climate Changed Civilization*. New York: Basic Books, 2004.

Freese, Barbara. *Coal: A Human History*. New York: Penguin, 2003.

Gore, Al. *An Inconvenient Truth*. Emmaus, PA: Rodale Press, 2006.

IPCC 2007. *Climate Change 2007: The Physical Science Basis—Contribution of Working Group I to the Fourth*

Earth's Changing Climate

Assessment Report of the Intergovernmental Panel on Climate Change. Edited by S. Solomon, D. Qin, M. Manning, Z. Chen, M. Marquis, K. B. Averyt, M. Tignor, and H. L. Miller. New York: Cambridge University Press, 2007.

Kolbert, Elizabeth. *Field Notes from a Catastrophe: Man, Nature, and Climate Change.* New York: Bloomsbury, 2006.

Stevens, William K. *The Change in the Weather: People, Weather, and the Science of Climate.* New York: Delta, 1999.

Tester, John. *Minnesota's Natural Heritage.* Minneapolis: University of Minnesota Press, 1995.

Wilson, E. O. *The Creation: An Appeal to Save Life on Earth.* New York: Norton, 2006.

Index

Pages in **boldface** are illustrations.

Earth's Changing Climate

About the Author

Christine Petersen lives near Minneapolis, Minnesota. Now a freelance writer and environmental educator, she spent the first few years of her career studying the behavior of North American bats. Later, as a science teacher, she helped develop environmental-education and service-learning curricula at an independent middle school. When she is not writing, Petersen conducts naturalist programs on bats and spends time with her young son. She enjoys snowshoeing, kayaking, photography, and birding. A member of the Society of Children's Book Writers, she is the author of more than three dozen books for young people.